FAMILY WALKS IN THE
FOREST OF BOWLAND

30 SHORT WALKS
IN AN AREA OF
OUTSTANDING NATURAL BEAUTY

JACK KEIGHLEY

ST. PAUL'S CHURCH, CATON-WITH-LITTLEDALE

WALK 5

FAMILY WALKS IN THE FOREST OF BOWLAND

an illustrated guide to thirty walks
of outstanding beauty and interest

by

J.Keighley

CICERONE PRESS

MILNTHORPE CUMBRIA

Also by *J Keighley*

WALKS IN THE YORKSHIRE DALES
ISBN 1 85284 034 X

**WALKS IN THE YORKSHIRE DALES
BOOK TWO**

ISBN 1 85284 065 X

**WALKS IN THE YORKSHIRE DALES
BOOK THREE**

ISBN 1 85284 085 4

WALKS IN LANCASHIRE WITCH COUNTRY

ISBN 1 85284 093 5

WALKS ON THE NORTH YORK MOORS

ISBN 1 85284 134 6

**WALKS ON THE NORTH YORK MOORS
BOOK TWO**

ISBN 1 85284 197 4

INTRODUCTION

The Forest of Bowland, a wild and sparsely-populated region of some 312 square miles, is undoubtedly the finest upland landscape that Lancashire has to offer, and was designated an Area of Outstanding Natural Beauty in 1964. It is a great dome of bare, windswept moors gashed by deep, desolate cloughs and verdant river valleys, sprinkled here and there with picturesque villages, tiny, secluded hamlets and lonely farmsteads.

The main mass of gritstone-capped fells may be regarded as one of England's last remaining wilderness areas. Here is grandeur and true solitude – a sweeping moorland terrain of rough, tussocky grass, weirdly-shaped peat hags and vast tracts of the heather which, in late summer, is one of the glories of Bowland. Clear, sparkling becks tumble and splash their merry way down to the valleys, where contented cows graze peacefully in lush riverside meadows, and where much ancient woodland still exists. The chief river of Bowland is the Hodder, and its upper valley – above Slaidburn and around Stocks Reservoir – is heavily forested. All of Bowland's rivers are beautiful, and the idyllic Hodder is the loveliest of them all.

Geologically Bowland belongs to the Pennines. The limestone around Slaidburn and Whitewell is the oldest rock in the area, and was formed some 350 million years ago at the bottom of a shallow, tropical sea. Aeons of time later the climate changed and the sea disappeared, to be replaced by a huge river laying down various sandy sediments in its delta. These deposits ultimately became the shales, sandstones and gritstones which are the predominant rocks of the Bowland uplands. The shape of the landscape we see today was fashioned 10,000 years ago by the glaciers and subsequent meltwaters of the last Ice Age.

There is little evidence of the presence of prehistoric man in Bowland. The best-known ancient site is an early-Bronze Age (about 1800 BC) village in Bleasdale, and Fairy Holes, a cave near Whitewell, yielded relics of similar vintage when excavated in 1946. Neither is there any sign of occupation by the Romans, though they did build a military road across the region to link their fort at Ribchester with the one at Burrow in Lonsdale. Anglo-Saxon invaders of the 6th and 7th C established settlements in the limestone areas, and in their wake came the Vikings to colonise some of the higher ground.

The Normans considerably depopulated the district. In addition to making massive land grants to monastic houses they also enforced 'forest laws', so that much of the region became a hunting forest for the nobility. The 13th C saw the appearance of many cattle farms (vaccaries), and also a marked decrease in the deer population. Two huge deer parks (Leagram and Radholme) were established, but both had been abandoned by the 16th C. It was during the Middle Ages that trade routes through Bowland developed. A complex network of green roads linked the hamlets, monastic granges and farmsteads, and along them plodded the packhorses burdened with such commodities as wool, salt, grain, lime and coal.

The industrial revolution touched Bowland only superficially, and the few village mills which still remain now look quaintly incongruous in their rural surroundings. A far more considerable and lasting impact on the landscape and economy of the area was made by the great 'sporting' estates which were set up during the 18th/19th C for grouse and pheasant shooting.

5

Nature-lovers will find themselves in Paradise when they visit Bowland. Rare flowering plants, mosses and grasses are to be found both on the moorland and in old hay meadows which have never come under the plough. The solitude of the moors makes them an attractive breeding-ground for such upland birds as ring ouzel, lapwing, golden plover, curlew, short-eared owl, merlin and peregrine falcon. The aforementioned plantations around Stocks Reservoir provide an ideal habitat for goshawk, sparrowhawk, various owls and smaller species such as goldcrest, siskin, pied flycatcher and assorted tits. The reservoir's island is a nesting-site for waders, waterfowl and raucous colonies of gulls. The shy sika deer roams the region, preferring woodland cover to the open fell, and the larger red deer – once abundant – is showing signs of re-establishing itself.

Though generally regarded as a remote area, the Forest of Bowland is in fact encircled by good roads, and access is easy from the A65 (Skipton-Settle-Ingleton), A59 (Skipton-Clitheroe-Preston) and M6, which skirts the region's western boundary.

When you have completed all the walks in this book you will have tramped over sombre moors, sauntered through silent forests and shady woodland glades, meandered along sun-kissed river-banks, ambled across flowery meadows and breezy upland pastures, strolled down leafy lanes, stumbled through glutinous quagmires and slimy peat hags, gazed in admiration from breathtaking viewpoints, fallen over decrepit stiles and cursed the author for getting you lost. You will have seen this Arcadian countryside in all its facets and, possibly – if you've walked through four seasons – in all its moods. Inevitably you will have fallen in love with 'Bolland'. It's that sort of place.

Happy Walking

JKeighley
January 1997

ABOUT THIS BOOK

THE WALKS All the walks described in this book are circular, and begin at a place where a car may be parked without causing an obstruction. They are fairly uniform in length, an average of 6½ miles making them half-day rather than full-day excursions. The routes, which adhere to public rights-of-way and permissive paths, should be free from serious difficulty and well within the capability of reasonably fit and agile walkers.

Although the author has personally researched and walked all these routes, it must be pointed out that changes will occur quite frequently. Walkers may expect to encounter new stiles and fences and possibly diversions – either temporary or permanent. In such cases please note and obey legitimate waymarks and signs.

THE MAPS The strip-maps show all relevant route-finding features, and great care has been taken to ensure accuracy, although for the sake of clarity there is deliberate distortion of scale in depicting routes along, for example, narrow lanes or through farmyards. In the Route Directions any mention of a stile, gate or footbridge means that it is used, unless otherwise stated. The maps and route directions together should suffice to make it quite clear to you how you've got lost. It is, however, strongly recommended that an Ordnance Survey map be carried, as this will add interest and enable the walker to identify distant features not mentioned in the text. The Outdoor Leisure Map 41 (Forest of Bowland and Ribblesdale) covers all the walks except Nº 24 (Stonyhurst and Longridge Fell). In addition the area is covered by seven maps in the Pathfinder Series, and these are indicated by code letters as follows :-

	SHEET		WALKS
A	637	BURTON-IN-KENDAL	5 11 18 21 30
B	650	HIGH BENTHAM AND CLAPHAM	3 13 17 21
C	659	GALGATE AND DOLPHINHOLME	6 9 11 15 27
D	660	SLAIDBURN AND FOREST OF BOWLAND	1 4 6 8 10 15 17 19 20 22 23 25 29
E	668	GARSTANG	2 7 12 15 26 28
F	669	CLITHEROE AND CHIPPING	2 4 14 15 16 20 22 24
G	680	LONGRIDGE AND GREAT HARWOOD	24

7

WALKING IN BOWLAND

Bowland has traditionally been somewhat hostile towards walkers. There is a good network of footpaths on the low ground, but very few rights-of-way over the high fells. The access situation in Bowland is an ongoing wrangle and, despite constant pressure from the Ramblers' Association, vast expanses of these splendid moors remain barred to walkers.

ACCESS AREAS Lancashire County Council has negotiated agreements with some landowners to provide two Access Areas where the walker is free to wander as he/she pleases. One Access Area is centred upon Clougha Pike, whilst the other is on the fells above Chipping (Fairsnape, Wolf Fell and Saddle Fell). In addition, there is a narrow ACCESS STRIP running from Grit Fell to Tarnbrook and taking in Bowland's highest point (Ward's Stone 1836 feet). These areas have certain bye-laws and access restrictions which MUST be observed, notably :-

- Areas (except Fairsnape) and Strip may be closed for grouse-shooting from 12th. August for a limited number of days (not Sundays) until 12th. December.

- NO DOGS (except on Wolf Fell), fires or stoves.

- Areas and Strip may be closed at short notice at times of high fire risk.

Countryside Rangers patrol the Access Areas and will give advice and information. If in doubt before setting off from home, contact Lancashire Countryside Services (01772 - 264709).

SOME GENERAL ADVICE

- Many of the routes in this book cross agricultural land, and farmers will not welcome inconsiderate visitors. When crossing fields keep closely to paths, and walk in single file across meadowland. Avoid climbing walls, and securely close all gates behind you (unless they are obviously meant to be left open).

- Cars must not be parked where they obstruct field gates or cause damage to grass verges. Lock your car and hide from view any attractive or valuable articles (or take them with you).

- Some of the walks described in this book cross high, exposed moorland terrain where weather conditions may be less pleasant than at valley level. Should the weather turn nasty, don't hesitate to call it a day and return by the route along which you came.

- Before setting out, let others know exactly where you're going (especially if you're walking alone).

- When walking along a motor-road walk on the RIGHT to face oncoming traffic. The exception to this is on approaching a blind right-hand bend, when you should cross to the left for a clearer view.

CLOTHING AND EQUIPMENT

Boots or strong, comfortable shoes are essential (on the high moors and in winter BOOTS are the ONLY suitable footwear). A windproof jacket or anorak (preferably with a hood) will be needed. Thick, heavy sweaters are not recommended — two or three lightweight layers are warmer and more adaptable to changing conditions. Denim is not at all suitable. In cold weather a woollen hat or cap will prevent the loss of a great deal of body heat. A rucsac is needed. A small 'daysac' with a capacity of about 20-25 litres would be adequate for any of these walks. The author's rucsac will always contain the following items :-

● waterproof cagoule and overtrousers ● small first-aid kit ● spare laces ● large-scale o.s. map ● compass ● whistle ● plastic bottle for cold drink and/or flask for coffee or soup ● a high-calorie snack (e.g. chocolate or crisps) ● windproof lighter for getting the old briar going (the alternative being about ten boxes of matches).

In very wet, muddy conditions gaiters are an asset, once you've managed to get them on (it helps if you're a contortionist). A walking-stick is a matter of personal preference. Some walkers wouldn't be seen dead with one, but the author finds a knobstick useful for very steep, slippery descents, fording streams, beating down nettles, discouraging aggressive animals and testing potentially boggy ground prior to sinking in up to the knees.

CHILDREN

When taking children on country walks some thought must be given to the distance and the type of terrain involved. Until you're sure of the child's capabilities, keep the distances short. Most of the walks in this book would probably be too much for a child under the age of five. As a rough rule-of-thumb, a child should be able to manage about a mile for each year of his age after his fifth birthday. Children should be warmly clothed and well shod. One cannot always afford to buy expensive boots for growing feet, but at least the child should have strong shoes or close-fitting wellingtons. On no account should young children be allowed to wander off beyond the range of vision of responsible adults, and extreme care and control must be exercised in the vicinity of crags, quarries, old mine workings and motor-roads.

DOGS

Some of my readers have suggested that I indicate how suitable the walks are for dogs. This is not easy, as a lot depends on the dog. The two main problems are livestock and stiles — particularly ladder-stiles. Dogs should be kept under close control at all times, and MUST be on a lead in the proximity of farms and farm livestock. You will be lucky to complete any of these walks without encountering cattle and/or sheep. A lead should also be used when walking on motor-roads or on moorland during nesting-time (April-June). Some large, agile dogs are able to scramble over ladder-stiles, but small dogs need to be lifted over, and this can sometimes be awkward if you're walking alone. If your dog is big, fat and rheumaticky then you have problems. Best places for dogs are high, open ground and woodland ; worst are motor-roads and lowland pastures.

THE WALKS

No		MILES	No		MILES
1	STOCKS-IN-BOWLAND	6½	16	LITTLE BOWLAND	8
2	FAIR SNAPE FELL AND PARLICK	5½	17	CROSS OF GREET BRIDGE	6
3	THE UPPER HINDBURN VALLEY	6½	18	LITTLEDALE	6½
4	MELLOR KNOLL AND BURHOLME	6½	19	CROASDALE	6
5	BROOKHOUSE AND CLAUGHTON	6¾	20	HARROP	9½
6	TARNBROOK AND MARSHAW	6½	21	ROEBURNDALE	5½
7	BEACON FELL AND THE RIVER BROCK	6¾	22	BOLTON-BY-BOWLAND	7¼
8	THE HEART OF BOWLAND	7	23	BEATRIX	5
9	JUBILEE TOWER	4½	24	STONYHURST AND LONGRIDGE FELL	8¼
10	SLAIDBURN AND NEWTON	4½	25	WHELP STONE CRAG	5½
11	CLOUGHA PIKE	4½	26	CALDER VALE	5¾
12	NICKY NOOK	6¾	27	AROUND ABBEYSTEAD	5
13	THE GREAT STONE OF FOURSTONES	5	28	BLEASDALE	5
14	WHITEWELL AND BROWSHOLME	6¾	29	WHITENDALE	7½
15	FIENDSDALE	9¼	30	LUNESIDE PATHS	7¼

ROAD MAP OF THE AREA
SHOWING THE
STARTING POINTS
OF THE 30 WALKS
DESCRIBED IN THIS BOOK

1 SLAIDBURN
2 FELL FOOT
3 IVAH
4 DUNSOP BRIDGE
5 BULL BECK CAR PARK
6 ABBEYSTEAD
7 BEACON FELL CAR PARK
8 LANGDEN INTAKE
9 JUBILEE TOWER
10 SLAIDBURN
11 BIRK BANK CAR PARK
12 SCORTON
13 HIGH BENTHAM
14 WHITEWELL
15 LANGDEN INTAKE
16 CHIPPING
17 BOWLAND KNOTTS
18 LITTLE CRAGG CAR PARK
19 SLAIDBURN
20 WALLOPER WELL
21 BARKIN BRIDGE
22 BOLTON - BY - BOWLAND
23 DUNSOP BRIDGE
24 KEMPLE END
25 TOSSIDE
26 CALDER VALE
27 ABBEYSTEAD
28 BEACON FELL (QUARRY) CAR PARK
29 WOOD HOUSE LANE
30 CROOK O' LUNE CAR PARK

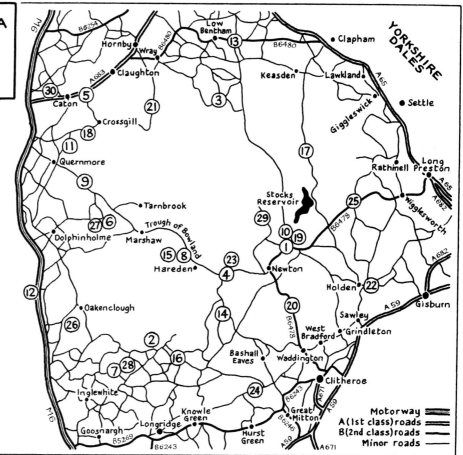

1 STOCKS-IN-BOWLAND — 6½ MILES

P Slaidburn. Car park and toilets at E end of village. Map ref: 713 523

ROUTE DIRECTIONS

① Up road into village and R at War Memorial. ② At far side of bridge R through swing-gate. Follow stream for about 100yds then veer L up past wall corner to ladder-stile. Forward alongside wall on L. ③ R down farm road, cross bridge, turn L and follow track to farm. ④ Follow track to R of buildings then R up to LH of three gates (wm). Forward with wall on R, straight on alongside wood and into enclosed green track. ⑤ At end of track cross ladder-stile and forward to gate just to R of wood. Follow edge of wood to gate into farm, pass to L of house and out along drive. ⑥ Straight on along tarmac road. Where it bends R turn R (FP sign) and follow tiny stream down to wall-stile. Bear L to pass to L of barn and follow cart-track. ⑦ At farm road you will see step-stile in wall directly ahead. Make your way round to it via bridge on L. Forward up open pasture, aiming slightly to R of distant farmhouse to locate stile near small building in wall corner. Forward to cross tiny stream, then bear L through gap in fence (wm) and up to gate at L of house. ⑧ R along road. ⑨ R over cattle-grid and down farm road. ⑩ Walk into farmyard and turn L to pass to L of house. Out into field and up to metal gate at its far RH corner. Straight on past RH edge of wood, over wall-stile and forward with fence on L. ⑪ Approaching end of field bear R to cross fence-stile and maintain direction to locate stile (not obvious) almost in wall corner. Over it turn L alongside wall and cross fence-stile and ditch to reach farm road. ⑫ R for a (cont. R)

(cont.) few paces to wm post and slant L up to wall-stile. Bear ½ R, crossing ditch to small ladder-stile. Maintain direction across next field to gate, then follow wall on L to step-stile under hawthorn. ⑬ Keep to LH side of field. Cross fence-stile near corner, turn R to cross another, then descend to pass L of Nissen hut to gate. R over bridge to car park.

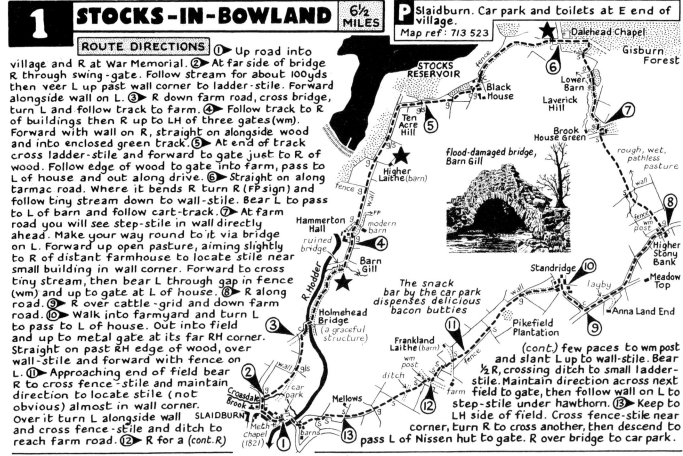

STOCKS RESERVOIR

Dalehead Chapel

Gisburn Forest

Black House

Lower Barn

Laverick Hill

Brook House Green

Ten Acre Hill

rough, wet, pathless pasture

flood-damaged bridge, Barn Gill

Higher Laithe (barn)

Hammerton Hall

modern barn

ruined bridge

Barn Gill

Higher Stony Bank

Meadow Top

Standridge

layby

Anna Land End

R. Hodder

The snack bar by the car park dispenses delicious bacon butties

Pikefield Plantation

Holmehead Bridge (a graceful structure)

Frankland Laithe (barn)

wm post

ditch

farm

wall

car park

Croasdale Brook

SLAIDBURN

Meth Chapel (1821)

Mellows

barns

Easy walking in lowland pastures. No steep gradients. 1 mile on motor roads. Compass useful in mist between points ⑦ and ⑧. Second half of walk (beyond chapel) likely to be muddy after rain. 3 ladder-stiles (2 with adjacent gates) and several awkward wall-stiles. Not a good walk for dogs.

Hammerton Hall

Hammerton Hall is a noble and sturdy Elizabethan mansion with a wonderfully diverse display of mullioned windows. Above the door of the three-storey central porch is a huge bay window which would once have been used by the women of the house whilst engaged in spinning and needlework. The present building stands on the site of a 12th. C. hall which was the original home of the Hammertons, powerful and rich landowners with a reputation for philanthropy and generosity. Alas, the Hammertons are no more, their downfall being brought about by their involvement in the Pilgrimage of Grace (1536), a protest against the dissolution of the lesser monasteries. The then head of the family, Sir Stephen Hammerton, was tried for treason, found guilty, and subsequently hanged and beheaded.

HAMERTON

STOCKS RESERVOIR

Major construction work on this huge reservoir began in 1922, but prior to this date a great deal of preliminary work had been carried out. Reconstruction of the road from Long Preston allowed heavy vehicles to reach a depot at Tosside, from where a 5-mile-long 3' gauge railway was laid to the site of the dam. Here a 'construction village' was erected to accommodate some 400 workmen and their families. This temporary settlement had its own canteen, cinema, recreation hall, offices and workshops. Stocks Reservoir was officially opened by H.R.H. Prince George K.G. on 5th. July 1932. It is two miles long with a surface area of almost 350 acres, and its water supplies the Fylde and Blackpool district. With its tiny island and numerous bays and inlets, the reservoir is more visually attractive than many of its ilk. Stocks is popular with anglers, and ornithologists will find much of interest throughout the year. The island has a raucous colony of black-headed gulls, which breed here, along with a few pairs of ducks and the occasional pair of Canada geese. In spring and autumn the reservoir and its margins attract passage waders, whilst in winter a wide variety of wildfowl may be seen on the water. The rare osprey and black tern have been seen here.

A LOST VILLAGE

lies beneath these waves, for when the reservoir was created its waters engulfed the hamlet of STOCKS-IN-BOWLAND. On the lake bed, close to the island, are the remains of its cottages, inn, shops and school. The church was dismantled, and in 1938 its stones were used to build a replacement – the tiny Church of St. James. More commonly referred to as Dalehead Chapel, it stands in a remote and peaceful setting on the edge of the vast Gisburn Forest.

The GOOSANDER is one of several species of waterfowl to be seen wintering at Stocks

Dalehead Chapel

FOR NOTES ON SLAIDBURN SEE WALK 19

O.S. MAP D

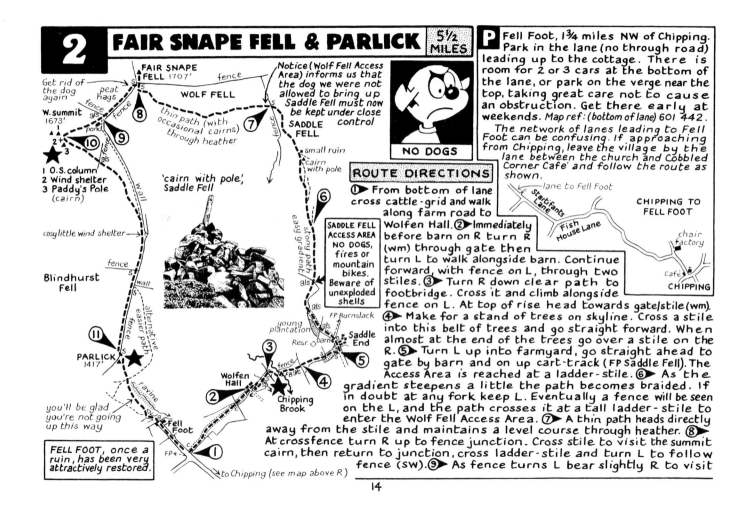

2 FAIR SNAPE FELL & PARLICK — 5½ MILES

P Fell Foot, 1¾ miles NW of Chipping. Park in the lane (no through road) leading up to the cottage. There is room for 2 or 3 cars at the bottom of the lane, or park on the verge near the top, taking great care not to cause an obstruction. Get there early at weekends. Map ref: (bottom of lane) 601 442.

The network of lanes leading to Fell Foot can be confusing. If approaching from Chipping, leave the village by the lane between the church and Cobbled Corner Café and follow the route as shown.

NO DOGS

ROUTE DIRECTIONS

① From bottom of lane cross cattle-grid and walk along farm road to Wolfen Hall. ② Immediately before barn on R turn R (wm) through gate then turn L to walk alongside barn. Continue forward, with fence on L, through two stiles. ③ Turn R down clear path to footbridge. Cross it and climb alongside fence on L. At top of rise head towards gate/stile (wm). ④ Make for a stand of trees on skyline. Cross a stile into this belt of trees and go straight forward. When almost at the end of the trees go over a stile on the R. ⑤ Turn L up into farmyard, go straight ahead to gate by barn and on up cart-track (FP Saddle Fell). The Access Area is reached at a ladder-stile. ⑥ As the gradient steepens a little the path becomes braided. If in doubt at any fork keep L. Eventually a fence will be seen on the L, and the path crosses it at a tall ladder-stile to enter the Wolf Fell Access Area. ⑦ A thin path heads directly away from the stile and maintains a level course through heather. ⑧ At crossfence turn R up to fence junction. Cross stile to visit the summit cairn, then return to junction, cross ladder-stile and turn L to follow fence (SW). ⑨ As fence turns L bear slightly R to visit

Map labels

Get rid of the dog again

FAIR SNAPE FELL 1707'

WOLF FELL

fence

peat hags

fence

W. summit 1673'

2
3
1 O.S. column
2 Wind shelter
3 Paddy's Pole (cairn)

⑧ thin path (with occasional cairns) through heather

Notice (Wolf Fell Access Area) informs us that the dog we were not allowed to bring up Saddle Fell must now be kept under close control

⑦

SADDLE FELL

small ruin

cairn with pole

⑥

cosy little wind shelter

'cairn with pole', Saddle Fell

fence

Blindhurst Fell

wall

SADDLE FELL ACCESS AREA NO DOGS, fires or mountain bikes. Beware of unexploded shells

easy gradient stony path

gls

FP Burnslack

young plantation

Resr.

barn

Saddle End

alternative easier path

fence

⑪ PARLICK 1417'

③
fence
FB gls
④
⑤

Wolfen Hall

②

Chipping Brook

ravine

you'll be glad you're not going up this way

Fell Foot

FP ←

①

FELL FOOT, once a ruin, has been very attractively restored.

to Chipping (see map above R)

lane to Fell Foot

Startifants Lane

Fish House Lane

CHIPPING TO FELL FOOT

chair factory

café

CHIPPING

14

👣 Moderately strenuous hill-walking, with 1250' of ascent on steady rather than steep gradients. Some peat hags and heavy ground in the vicinity of the true summit of Fair Snape Fell (Point⑧); otherwise generally firm going. Most of the walk is on good tracks and paths, but in mist it would be useful to have a compass handy. No motor-roads. 5 ladder-stiles (2 with adjacent gates).

2

W. summit (*in mist it would be better to omit this detour and stay with the fence/wall on the L*). ⑩ ▶ From O.S. column walk to L of wind-shelter to locate path heading S.E. towards ridge-wall. Follow wall down to col and stay on RH side of it to climb Parlick. ⑪ ▶ Cross ladder-stile at summit and walk past 'cairn' to a very steep path, with ravine on L, descending to lane at Fell Foot.

The ladder-stile at Point ⑦ giving access to Wolf Fell.

WOLFEN HALL
, once the old manor house of Chipping, has its origins in the 13th.C. In those far-off days it was a lookout post to warn of the presence of roaming packs of wolves which posed a threat to domestic livestock. It has now been completely rebuilt and, though undeniably a smart house, retains none of its original character.

CHIPPING BROOK
once provided power for several watermills in and around Chipping. We cross it at a footbridge in a peaceful and secluded valley – a place of considerable charm (but too early yet to stop for a picnic).

⭐ SADDLE FELL, WOLF FELL, FAIR SNAPE FELL AND PARLICK
ARE COLLECTIVELY KNOWN AS THE BLEASDALE FELLS, AND THE LATTER PAIR ARE TWO OF THE BEST-KNOWN AND MOST-CLIMBED HILLS IN BOWLAND. THE TRUE SUMMIT OF FAIR SNAPE (POINT ⑧) IS THE HIGHEST POINT OF THESE BLEAK FELLS, AND PRESENTS A WEIRD LANDSCAPE OF PEAT TORS AND HAGS DRAPED IN HEATHER AND BILBERRY. MUCH MORE POPULAR WITH WALKERS IS THE WESTERN SUMMIT (POINT ⑩), FURNISHED WITH AN ORDNANCE SURVEY COLUMN, TWO LARGE CAIRNS AND A STURDY CRUCIFORM WIND-SHELTER. FROM THIS FINE VANTAGE-POINT THERE ARE SPLENDID VIEWS ACROSS THE FYLDE PLAINS TO MORECAMBE BAY AND THE LAKELAND FELLS BEYOND. THE SHAPELY PARLICK APPEARS FROM ALMOST EVERY ANGLE AS A VERY GRACEFUL CONE, AND AGAIN IS A SUPERB VIEWPOINT, THOUGH THE SUMMIT IS NOT IN ITSELF PARTICULARLY INSPIRING. IN THE PAST PARLICK HAS BEEN USED AS A BEACON HILL AND AS A RALLYING-PLACE FOR LOCAL CATHOLICS – ESPECIALLY DURING THE JACOBITE REBELLIONS OF THE 18TH C. NOW IT IS A HAUNT OF GLIDERS AND HANG-GLIDERS, SOARING ON THE THERMALS RISING FROM THE VALLEY BELOW. THIS CAN BE A BIT UNNERVING FOR WALKERS, PARTICULARLY ON A SUNNY DAY, WHEN A SINISTER SHADOW SWEEPS ACROSS THE FELLSIDE AND A GHOSTLY HISS PROMPTS ONE TO GLANCE UPWARDS TO DISCOVER AN OTHERWISE SILENT AIRCRAFT JUST A FEW FEET ABOVE ONE'S HEAD.

the summit of Parlick

O.S. MAPS E F

P Ivah. There is a small layby at a sharp bend of the road between the hamlet and Stairend Bridge. Map ref : 655 639

NOTE BY USING THE LANE BETWEEN THE LAYBY AND STAIREND BRIDGE THE ROUTE MAY BE ADAPTED INTO TWO SEPARATE SHORT WALKS :– A. STAIREND – HELKS WOOD – LOWGILL – BRACKENBOTTOM – IVAH. 3 MILES B. SWANS – BOTTON HEAD – LOWER THRUSHGILL – STAIREND – IVAH. 4 MILES

ROUTE DIRECTIONS

① Walk up farm road (BW sign). Through LH gate into farmyard, pass between house and barn and straight on up slope to gate (wm). ② Forward alongside line of trees to descend to small, grassy bridge. In next field bear very slightly L to gateway, then keep L down big field to locate gate at bottom end of wall. Turn R down to footbridge. ③ Slant L up steep bank then past wall corner and head for farm. Straight on through yard and along drive. ④ Turn R along lane. Straight on at farm, passing to R of all buildings. ⑤ Enter yard of next farm and immediately turn R through gate. Descend L to footbridge, then follow fence/wall up steep hillside. ⑥ At top corner of field go R through gate and follow LH field boundary round below house and down to gate. Forward alongside fence, follow wall R to stile then head for building. ⑦ L up cart-track then R along tarmac lane. ⑧ Turn R along farm drive, then L to pass through little gate (looks private but isn't) at L of white house. Maintain dead-straight line through several fields, eventually keeping L of line of trees. When trees end descend to gate near river. ⑨ Go L along lane, cross tributary and turn R through gate. Follow sketchy track close to river. ⑩ Track passes through two gates then rises L to pass ruined barn. Straight on, following line of ruined wall then along obvious sunken path. ⑪ Just before reaching gate turn sharp R and descend past two telegraph poles to footbridge. ⑫ Cross field diagonally R to stile. Thin path climbs through wood to another stile. Continue up narrow field, take stile on L and straight up field to Lowgill. ⑬ L along road, cross bridge and turn R up lane (SP church). ⑭ Go along the church drive. Pass to R of church and through small gate in wall. Stay alongside wall for a few yards, then

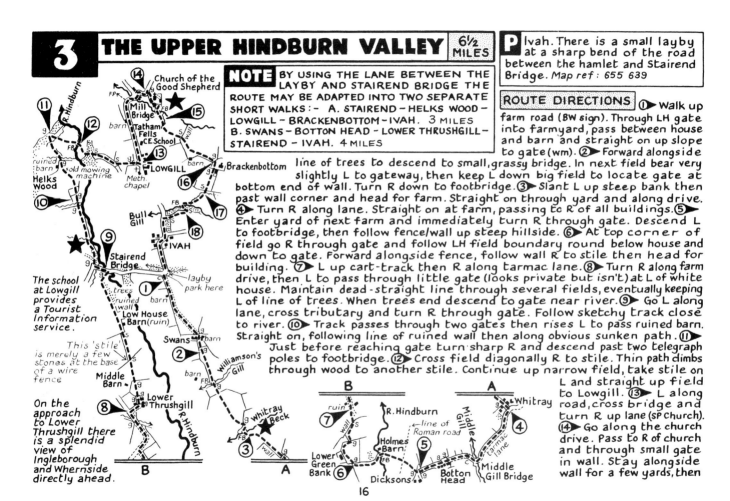

The school at Lowgill provides a Tourist Information service.

This 'stile' is merely a few stones at the base of a wire fence.

On the approach to Lower Thrushgill there is a splendid view of Ingleborough and Whernside directly ahead.

Mostly pathless sheep pastures. Dogs will be on lead most of the time. Quite strenuous, with lots of ups and downs and some steep gradients. ¾ mile on quiet motor roads. No ladder-stiles.

descend R by fence to footbridge. ⑮ Climb steep bank, and when farm appears away to L make for it, via step-stile in wall. ⑯ Enter farmyard and immediately turn R. Go through gate on R of large, modern barn and straight on along field to stile. ⑰ Follow ditch down to footbridge, then climb slightly L to stile. ⑱ Turn R and follow fence straight on to road. Turn L and keep straight on through hamlet to layby.

THE RIVER HINDBURN takes its name,
as does its neighbour the Roeburn, from the deer which once roamed these parts in large numbers. Tiny streams rushing down the bare slopes of Whitray Fell and Lythe Fell unite to flow swiftly along an ever-deepening and prettily wooded valley to the village of Wray, there to join forces with the aforementioned Roeburn. The Hindburn is entirely charming, and nowhere more so than between points ⑨ and ⑩ of our walk.

In the field between Dicksons and Holmes Barn we cross the line of a **ROMAN ROAD.** It is not discernible underfoot, but in certain conditions of light is just visible as a pale line on the fellside away to the left.

Whitray   *Lower Thrushgill*

Several of the farmhouses passed along the way display inscribed datestones, some of great antiquity. Examples are WHITRAY (1859), BOTTON HEAD (1666) and LOWER THRUSHGILL (1798).

CHURCH OF THE GOOD SHEPHERD, LOWGILL

An aptly dedicated church, for it serves the parish of Tatham, whose economy is largely dependent upon sheep. It was built 1885-7 (at a cost of £1,200!) to replace a church which had occupied the site for over 400 years.

LOWGILL is a remote and tranquil hamlet. Lowgill House sports an 18th.C. datestone and the Methodist Chapel has survived since 1866, but the Post Office has gone and the pub – the Rose and Crown – called 'Last Orders' in the late 1970s.

Keep a lookout for the **RED SQUIRREL** which, though now absent from many parts of England, survives in various Bowland localities. Red squirrels have lived in Britain since prehistoric times, but an epidemic disease has decimated their numbers.

O.S.MAP B

4 MELLOR KNOLL & BURHOLME — 6½ MILES

P Dunsop Bridge. Sizeable car park (and toilets) at east end of village. Map ref: 661 501

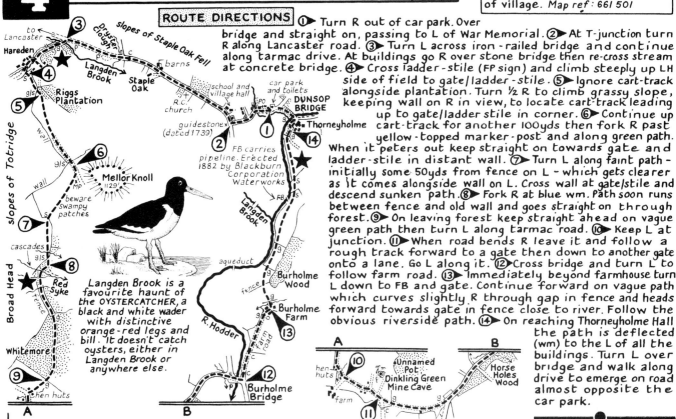

ROUTE DIRECTIONS

① Turn R out of car park. Over bridge and straight on, passing to L of War Memorial. ② At T-junction turn R along Lancaster road. ③ Turn L across iron-railed bridge and continue along tarmac drive. At buildings go R over stone bridge then re-cross stream at concrete bridge. ④ Cross ladder-stile (FP sign) and climb steeply up LH side of field to gate/ladder-stile. ⑤ Ignore cart-track alongside plantation. Turn ½ R to climb grassy slope, keeping wall on R in view, to locate cart-track leading up to gate/ladder stile in corner. ⑥ Continue up cart-track for another 100yds then fork R past yellow-topped marker-post and along green path. When it peters out keep straight on towards gate and ladder-stile in distant wall. ⑦ Turn L along faint path – initially some 50yds from fence on L – which gets clearer as it comes alongside wall on L. Cross wall at gate/stile and descend sunken path. ⑧ Fork R at blue wm. Path soon runs between fence and old wall and goes straight on through forest. ⑨ On leaving forest keep straight ahead on vague green path then turn L along tarmac road. ⑩ Keep L at junction. ⑪ When road bends R leave it and follow a rough track forward to a gate then down to another gate onto a lane. Go L along it. ⑫ Cross bridge and turn L to follow farm road. ⑬ Immediately beyond farmhouse turn L down to FB and gate. Continue forward on vague path which curves slightly R through gap in fence and heads forward towards gate in fence close to river. Follow the obvious riverside path. ⑭ On reaching Thorneyholme Hall the path is deflected (wm) to the L of all the buildings. Turn L over bridge and walk along drive to emerge on road almost opposite the car park.

Langden Brook is a favourite haunt of the OYSTERCATCHER, a black and white wader with distinctive orange-red legs and bill. It doesn't catch oysters, either in Langden Brook or anywhere else.

One steep climb of 400' up pathless pastures from Hareden to Mellor Knoll. Otherwise easy walking. 1¾ miles on motor roads. Compass useful in mist between points ⑥ and ⑦. Path through Whitemore Plantation can be very muddy. 4 ladder-stiles (3 with adjacent gates).

4

DUNSOP BRIDGE

Dunsop Bridge and Bridge Cottage

Though but a tiny village, Dunsop Bridge is one of the best-known and best-loved places in Bowland. It is well-known because of its situation at the southern entrance to the famous Trough, and popular because of its green, which is so idyllic that it is an almost obligatory stopping-place for passing motorists. This is a Paradise for children who, besides guzzling ice-cream from the nearby Post Office, may feed the friendly ducks and splosh about in the chuckling waters of the River Dunsop. A garage now stands where once was a blacksmith's forge. Dunsop Bridge grew up around this smithy, and increased in size during the 19th. C. as a result of lead-mining activity on the nearby fells. The little village now has a unique claim to fame in that the Ordnance Survey has declared that it stands at the exact centre of Great Britain. The telephone box (the 100,000th public payphone installed by BT) on the green commemorates the fact, its position having been calculated to a ten-figure grid reference. The mind boggles!

One third of a mile out of the village along the Trough road we pass the isolated R.C. CHURCH OF OUR LADY AND ST. HUBERT, built in 1864 by the Towneley family of Thorneyholme. St. Hubert, who died in 727 AD, is the patron saint of foresters.

HAREDEN was originally a grange of Kirkstall Abbey. It is now a picturesque grouping of houses and barns dating back to the 17th C. and set in a beautiful and peaceful valley (though the peace is likely to be shattered when you pass the kennels).

● **MELLOR KNOLL** IS KNOWN LOCALLY AS 'THE OLD MAN OF BOLLAND'. AT POINT ⑥ WE ARE WITHIN 200' OF ITS SUMMIT, BUT THERE IS NO RIGHT-OF-WAY THERETO.

● **BURHOLME BRIDGE** THROWS TWO GRACEFUL – ALBEIT IRREGULAR – 18TH C ARCHES ACROSS THE HODDER.

BURHOLME was, many centuries ago, a sizeable settlement with its own church. In the 1300s the Burholmians abandoned their village and emigrated to Whitewell, where the Radholme Deer Park had been established. The present farmhouse, with its massive gable chimney stack, incorporates two early 17th C buildings, though its frontage is 19th C. The last lap of our walk, from Burholme, is an easy saunter through riverside meadows.

one of the Mine Cave entrances

DINKLING GREEN MINE CAVE has several entrances at the base of a limestone cliff. It is fenced-off and unsafe to enter. UNNAMED POT is situated in a prominent shakehole at the corner of the nearby wood.

FOR NOTES ON THE RIVER HODDER AND THORNEYHOLME SEE WALK 23.

O.S. MAPS D F

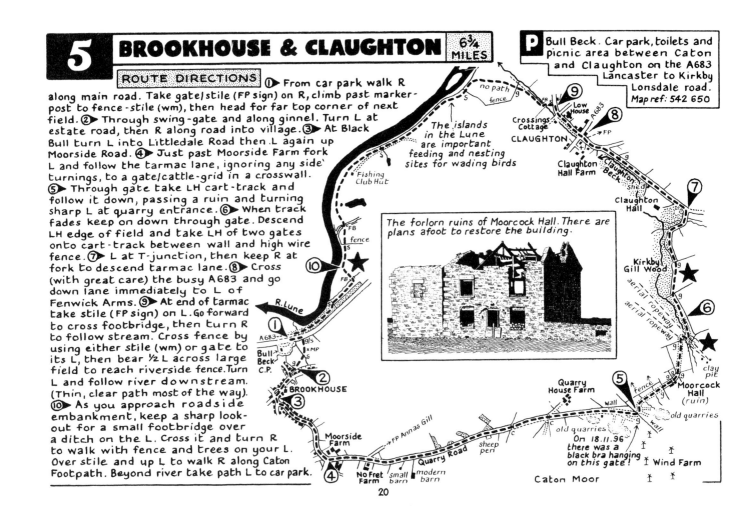

5 BROOKHOUSE & CLAUGHTON

6¾ MILES

ROUTE DIRECTIONS

①► From car park walk R along main road. Take gate/stile (FP sign) on R, climb past marker-post to fence-stile (wm), then head for far top corner of next field. **②►** Through swing-gate and along ginnel. Turn L at estate road, then R along road into village. **③►** At Black Bull turn L into Littledale Road then L again up Moorside Road. **④►** Just past Moorside Farm fork L and follow the tarmac lane, ignoring any side turnings, to a gate/cattle-grid in a crosswall. **⑤►** Through gate take LH cart-track and follow it down, passing a ruin and turning sharp L at quarry entrance. **⑥►** When track fades keep on down through gate. Descend LH edge of field and take LH of two gates onto cart-track between wall and high wire fence. **⑦►** L at T-junction, then keep R at fork to descend tarmac lane. **⑧►** Cross (with great care) the busy A683 and go down lane immediately to L of Fenwick Arms. **⑨►** At end of tarmac take stile (FP sign) on L. Go forward to cross footbridge, then turn R to follow stream. Cross fence by using either stile (wm) or gate to its L, then bear ½ L across large field to reach riverside fence. Turn L and follow river downstream. (Thin, clear path most of the way). **⑩►** As you approach roadside embankment, keep a sharp lookout for a small footbridge over a ditch on the L. Cross it and turn R to walk with fence and trees on your L. Over stile and up L to walk R along Caton Footpath. Beyond river take path L to car park.

P Bull Beck. Car park, toilets and picnic area between Caton and Claughton on the A683 Lancaster to Kirkby Lonsdale road. Map ref: 542 650

The islands in the Lune are important feeding and nesting sites for wading birds

The forlorn ruins of Moorcock Hall. There are plans afoot to restore the building.

no path fence

Low House

Crossings Cottage
CLAUGHTON

Claughton Hall Farm

Claughton Hall

Kirkby Gill Wood

aerial ropeway

aerial ropeway

clay pit

Moorcock Hall (ruin)

old quarries

Fishing Club Hut

R.Lune

A683

Bull Beck C.P.

BROOKHOUSE

Moorside Farm

No Fret Farm

small barn

modern barn

FP Annas Gill

Quarry Road

sheep pen

Quarry House Farm

wall

old quarries

On 18.11.96 there was a black bra hanging on this gate!

Wind Farm

Caton Moor

20

Easy walking, with no steep gradients. Between points ② and ⑤ (the highest point of the walk at 870') there is a two-mile walk on tarmac, but it's virtually traffic-free and provides wonderful views. No ladder-stiles. The 1¼-mile riverside section can be juicy after prolonged rain. The walk has an abundance of interesting features, and route-finding couldn't be simpler – only a genius could get lost on this one.

❖ ST. PAUL'S CHURCH ❖
CATON-WITH-LITTLEDALE

This splendid Parish Church stands in the attractive village of Brookhouse. It is believed that a church existed here as early as the 13th C., and that it was rebuilt in Henry VIII's time. Apart from the 55 feet high, 16th C. tower, the present building dates from c1865. Built into the west wall is a Norman doorway (*illustrated*), a remnant of the old church. Its sculptured arch depicts the 'Temptation of Eden'. The top of the tree, the heads of Adam and Eve, the serpent and the figure of an animal are just discernible. The doorway is built up with sculptured stones found in the masonry of the former building in 1865. One of these stones is early 14th C., and displays a cross and sword, which were emblems of the crusaders.

CLAUGHTON HALL, an imposing house
with a lofty and somewhat forbidding façade, was moved stone by stone to its present site in the 1930s. Originally it stood down in the village by the church. Part of the house was left *in situ* and is now Claughton Hall Farm.

AT LOW HOUSE FARM WE CROSS THE LINE OF THE OLD NORTH-WESTERN RAILWAY, WHICH OPERATED 1849-1966. THE FINAL STAGE OF THE WALK IS ALONG THE TRACKBED.

O.S. MAP | **A**

Set into the parapet of the bridge by the Black Bull at Brookhouse is a large stone with a hollowed-out top. This is the **PLAGUE STONE**, where those contaminated with the 'pestilence' left money in exchange for food. The hollow would contain vinegar to 'sterilize' the coins. Bubonic plague swept across Europe in the years 1348-50, killing nearly one-third of the population. The disease was transmitted by fleas from the black rat, though this was not known at the time. There were recurrent outbreaks up to the late 17th C., and the epidemic which raged in England in 1665 wiped out whole villages and one-tenth of London's citizens.

Fenwick Arms, Claughton
An excellent watering-hole

Just below Moorcock Hall we pass a large quarry where shale and clay is obtained for the brickworks at Claughton. The material is transported down Kirkby Gill in buckets on an aerial ropeway. Look out for a bucket sporting elephant's ears and the name DUMBO.

ST. CHAD'S CHURCH, Claughton, has the oldest dated bell in England (1296).

ROUTE DIRECTIONS

① Walk back through the gateposts and turn R up road. ② Where road bends L go forward through gate (wm), pass to L of garage and cross lawn to ladder-stile (wm). Forward with wood on R, and as wall curves away R keep straight on towards farm. Through RH of two gates (with stile) then follow fence on L. Pass through gate (wm) and forward to stile onto road. ③ Along farm drive (wm) and at farmyard entrance turn R over ladder-stile (wm). Follow LH hedge to ladder-stile, then RH hedge round to another. ④ Head for barn, crossing stile (wm) in fence-corner en route. Pass to R of barn and follow RH field boundary. ⑤ At twin-stiles (gap and ladder) cross track to a ladder-stile. Straight on over three stiles to descend to river-bridge. ⑥ Cross bridge and up between walls to Tarnbrook. Walk R through hamlet to gate marked 'Gilberton' and follow farm track. ⑦ Fork R over cattle-grid. At river turn L to cross wooden footbridge, then forward to turn L along track by wall. Follow it to a yard between two barns. ⑧ Leave yard by gate on R and turn L (wm on tree) to climb to R of wall and trees. ⑨ At top of climb cross iron ladder-stile (wm) then ½ R to another ladder-stile. Maintain direction to another ladder-stile (wm), then aim for gate in wall between two woods. Descend green track to Tower Lodge. ⑩ Turn R along road. ⑪ At cattle-grid take ladder-stile on L to use concessionary path (see note above). ⑫ Where road turns R go forward over ladder-stile to follow hedge on L. At wall-corner straight on to LH end of wood. Follow edge of wood down to cross footbridge

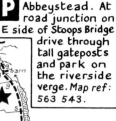

Abbeystead. At road junction on E side of Stoops Bridge drive through tall gateposts and park on the riverside verge. Map ref: 563 543.

NOTE: The concessionary path helpfully by-passes a narrow stretch of road, but has an awkward bit (marked * on the map) where the bank has collapsed, allowing the river to flow right up against the wall. No real problem in normal conditions, but if the river is in spate it would be prudent to stick to the road.

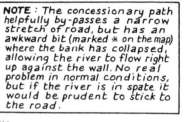

ALTERNATIVE START

If the small parking space at Stoops Bridge is full, the walk could be done from Tower Lodge – plenty of places to park on the roadside verge.

near Ouzel Thorn

Easy walking - no steep gradients. Mostly pathless pastures, reaching a height of 892' at point ⑨. Just under a mile on motor-roads (quite busy at weekends). 17 ladder-stiles (3 with adjacent gates). Beautiful views and typical Bowland scenery. Myriads of pheasants on final stages of walk.

then ladder-stile (with natty little dog-gate). Follow fence on L (ignore stile in it) to reach kissing-gate and footbridge. ⑬ ► Straight on, keeping roughly parallel with river, and look for flight of steps on L leading up to stile into wood. Follow fence on R, again keeping parallel with river. Thin path develops and passes a marker-post. ⑭ ► Just beyond large house descend to cross footbridge. Turn L to follow fence on L. Pass through iron gate and bear R to parking-place.

The barnyard at point ⑧

ABBEYSTEAD

is not visited on the walk, but you may feel disposed to undertake the short detour (200yds from Stoops Bridge) in order to view the pretty hamlet set in a wooded hollow at the heart of the Duke of Westminster's vast estate. You will find the scene utterly charming, with ducks waddling around amongst the daffodils which befringe the lovely old cottages. Some of the buildings display the coat-of-arms of the Sefton family. Opposite the tiny school is a fine pinfold, where stray animals were impounded in days of yore. The hamlet is named after an abbey founded here (possibly near the river confluence) in the 12th C. by a pioneering band of Cistercian monks from Furness. The venture, however, was not a success, and the abbey was soon abandoned. The beautiful lake which may be glimpsed through the trees was constructed in 1853 to provide water-power for textile mills at Dolphinholme. Abbeystead church lies almost a mile by road to the W of the hamlet (see Walk 27).

THE WYRE

IS THE ONLY RIVER WHICH FLOWS FROM BOWLAND TO THE SEA (ALL BOWLAND'S OTHER RIVERS EVENTUALLY JOIN EITHER THE LUNE OR THE RIBBLE). IT HAS TWO MAIN SOURCES. ONE COMES DOWN FROM TARNBROOK FELL AND IS KNOWN AS THE TARNBROOK WYRE, WHILST THE OTHER - THE MARSHAW WYRE - RISES ON BRENNAND FELL. THEY MEET JUST A FEW YARDS FROM THE STARTING-POINT OF THIS WALK AND FLOW ON TO ENTER THE SEA AT FLEETWOOD.

TARNBROOK

is only a tiny hamlet, having dwindled quite considerably in size since the days when it was a Quaker village renowned for the manufacture of fine quality rabbitskin and moleskin hats. The high moors above Tarnbrook are said to provide the best grouse shooting in England.

TOWER LODGE,

Tower Lodge

a familiar landmark to motorists using the Trough road, was the lodge for the now ruinous Wyresdale Tower, a former shooting-house. The unenclosed stretch of riverside road between Tower Lodge and MARSHAW is probably the best-known beauty spot in Bowland.

ABBEYSTEAD HALL, though Elizabethan in style, was built in 1886 by the Earl of Sefton. It is used as a summer residence by the Duke of Westminster and his family. Note the beautiful gardens.

O.S. MAPS C D

7 BEACON FELL & THE RIVER BROCK 6¾ MILES

P Beacon Fell Country Park, reached by a mazy network of narrow lanes but fortunately well-signposted. Use the main (Fell House) car park, which has toilets and a new Visitor Centre (under construction at time of writing - May 95) Map ref: 564 426.

TRY TO DO THIS WALK IN MAY, WHEN THE BLUEBELLS MAKE A SUPERB SHOW.

NOTE: Initially there are two Rivers Brock, one (West Brock) rising on Home House Fell and the other (East Brock) on Fair Snape Fell. The names 'East Brock' and 'West Brock' are unofficially bestowed by the author.

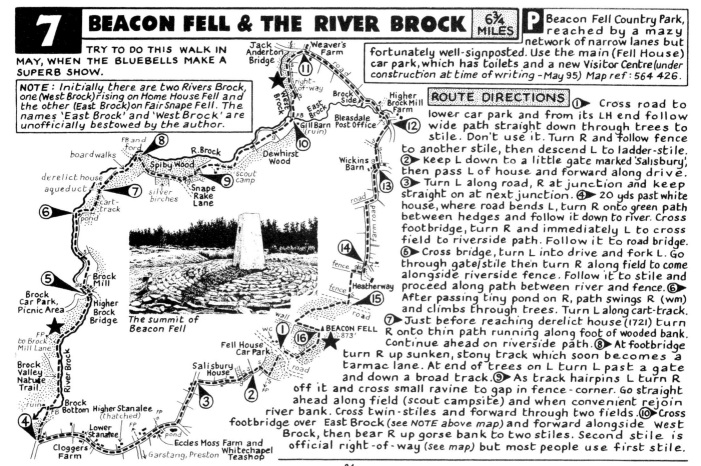

The summit of Beacon Fell

ROUTE DIRECTIONS

① Cross road to lower car park and from its LH end follow wide path straight down through trees to stile. Don't use it. Turn R and follow fence to another stile, then descend L to ladder-stile. ② Keep L down to a little gate marked 'Salisbury', then pass L of house and forward along drive. ③ Turn L along road, R at junction and keep straight on at next junction. ④ 20 yds past white house, where road bends L, turn R onto green path between hedges and follow it down to river. Cross footbridge, turn R and immediately L to cross field to riverside path. Follow it to road bridge. ⑤ Cross bridge, turn L into drive and fork L. Go through gate/stile then turn R along field to come alongside riverside fence. Follow it to stile and proceed along path between river and fence. ⑥ After passing tiny pond on R, path swings R (wm) and climbs through trees. Turn L along cart-track. ⑦ Just before reaching derelict house (1721) turn R onto thin path running along foot of wooded bank. Continue ahead on riverside path. ⑧ At footbridge turn R up sunken, stony track which soon becomes a tarmac lane. At end of trees on L turn L past a gate and down a broad track. ⑨ As track hairpins L turn R off it and cross small ravine to gap in fence-corner. Go straight ahead along field (scout campsite) and when convenient rejoin river bank. Cross twin-stiles and forward through two fields. ⑩ Cross footbridge over East Brock (see NOTE above map) and forward alongside West Brock, then bear R up gorse bank to two stiles. Second stile is official right-of-way (see map) but most people use first stile.

Near the end of the walk there is a steady climb of nearly 300' from Heatherway to the summit of Beacon Fell. Otherwise easy walking on lanes and good paths. 1¾ miles on motor-roads. 1½ miles of riverside walking. 1 ladder-stile.

Follow path along top of wood. ⑪▶ Walk R along road. ⑫▶ About 100yds beyond Post Office turn R up steps to stile (wm). Forward alongside fence to stile (wm) in crossfence. (*Waymarks here suggest crossing another stile on L to continue on LH side of fence, but entry to the farmyard this way may be blocked. O.S. map shows right-of-way remaining on RH side.*) Pass through farmyard. ⑬▶ Turn R along road then L up farm road (FP sign). ⑭▶ Straight on (wm) up drive to Heatherway. When drive bends L take stile (wm) on R. Follow fence for 100yds, and at wm turn L to climb straight up field to stile and road above. ⑮▶ Take a few steps R along road, then go L up path climbing diagonally through forest. On emerging, cross wide track and straight on up open hillside. At wall turn L to climb to O.S. column at summit. ⑯▶ Turn R at summit to follow broad path, soon accompanied by wall on R, down through trees and eventually turning R to car park.

➡ **WHEN LEAVING THE CAR PARK DON'T FORGET THAT THE ROAD CIRCLING THE FELL IS A CLOCKWISE ONE-WAY SYSTEM**

BEACON FELL

, a small, isolated hill on the S.W. fringe of Bowland, was opened in October 1970 as one of Lancashire's first Country Parks. A cycleway and numerous short walks have been laid out to enable its many visitors to enjoy a variety of environments ranging from silent, gloomy forest to colourful moorland, and a view indicator at the summit picks out the main features of the superb panorama. Most of the trees are conifers such as sitka spruce, Scots pine and larch, interspersed with various deciduous species including oak, rowan, silver birch, alder and maple. Fell House car park occupies the site of a former farmhouse.

SPIBY WOOD, shown as 'BOGGY WOOD' on O.S. maps, has been renamed in memory of the late Cyril Spiby, a well-known local rambler and guidebook writer.

THE BROCK VALLEY, a sylvan paradise much loved by local ramblers, has a rich variety of woodland and aquatic plants. Red Campion, Water Avens, Wood Avens (Herb Bennet), Stitchwort, Foxglove, Ramsons, Butterbur, Comfrey, Yellow Iris and Meadow-sweet are some of the species which will be noted by the botanist.
Dippers, wagtails and other riverside birds abound, and if you're very fortunate you may catch a glimpse of a kingfisher.

The striking façade of ECCLES MOSS FARM. The building is over 300 years old and is one of several attractive houses passed on the early stages of the walk.

O.S. MAP E

P Langden Intake. Parking area (usually with mobile snack bar) where the Langden Water Works drive leaves the Dunsop Bridge – Lancaster (Trough) road 1¾ miles NW of Dunsop Bridge. *Map ref: 632 511.* Take care not to obstruct the drive.

A

park and start here —

① Sykes Nab

Langden Water Works

Staple Oak Fell

B

Optional finish. See note on next page.

⑪

concessionary (Water Auth) path

Smelt Mill Cottages

⑥ Brennand Farm

Lower Brennand

Whitendale Farm

Brennand River

Whitendale River

ROUTE DIRECTIONS

⑨ Dryster Clough

⑦

Closes

barns

Brennand Stones

small ruin

Whins Brow

fence

Ouster Rake

wall post

Hind Clough

post

Foot Holme shed

birth of the River Dunsop

① From Water Works drive entrance walk L along motor road, passing farm on R then kiln on L.
② Go R through gate by barn and ascend rough cart-track, passing above (not through) plantation. Follow track past ruined farm and into short, enclosed section. ③ At end of enclosed section stay with wall on R until it drops away, then keep straight on along thin path, passing a couple of posts. Path is very faint in places but is always rising gently, and eventually reaches gate in wall. ④ Path climbs steeply above LH side of shaly ravine, faint initially but more distinct as height is gained. It eventually comes alongside fence on R and runs on to gate/stile in crossfence. ⑤ Continue forward on thin path which soon swings L to suddenly reach a tremendous declivity. Clear path slants down steep fell-side to gate at wall-corner. Continue forward on thin path, soon veering R to descend to farm. Cross ladder-stile into farmyard. ⑥ Turn R and follow farm road down valley, keeping R at a Y-junction. ⑦ Just before reaching cattle-grid and farm turn R into field (no path). Cross to stile into chicken-runs and forward through iron gate in wall. Follow wall on L, and when it turns away to barns veer R to gate (BW sign). ⑧ Walk R

⑩ Langden Brook ⑧

Trough House (ruin)

young plantation

posts

wall posts

highest point of walk 1410'

shaly ravine

⑤

fence

③ ④

Trough and Lancaster

fence

wall

plantation

Rams Clough

② Trough Barn

Losterdale Brook

quarries and kiln

waterworks

Sykes Farm

A

The roadside kiln

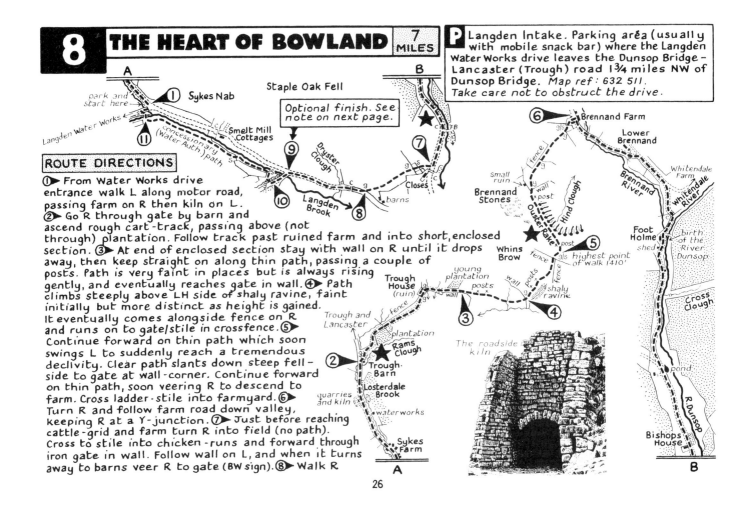

Cross Clough

pond

R. Dunsop

Bishops House

B

26

Varied terrain. 2 miles of moderately strenuous hill-walking on rough tracks and thin paths rising to just over 1400'. 2½ miles down a tarmac (but scenic) farm road. 1 mile on motor-roads. 1 ladder-stile (with adjacent gate). Compass useful in mist between points ③ and ⑥. Vertigo sufferers may be unhappy on Ouster Rake. Not recommended in severe wintry conditions.

8

along road. ⑨▶ Turn L over iron-railed bridge and along lane. ⑩▶ When trees on R end go through gate on R, cross stream and turn R down to stile. Walk upstream alongside wall, cross wooden stile and continue along riverside field. ⑪▶ Cross iron bridge to stile and turn R along drive

●—●—●

NOTE - OPTIONAL FINISH From point ⑧ the walk may be completed simply by following the motor-road up to Langden. This, however, can be a nerve-racking experience on summer weekends and Bank Holidays when the narrow road becomes congested with trippers' transport. In particular, the area seems to be a Mecca for hell-bent motor-cyclists astride enormous, noisy and lethal-looking machines. Fortunately the risk of being mown down can be considerably reduced by effecting an early escape down to a Water Authority concessionary footpath alongside Langden Brook which provides an easier, safer and infinitely more pleasurable finish to the walk. The lively LANGDEN BROOK has a wealth of birdlife. In addition to the oystercatcher (see Walk 4), look out for the GREY WAGTAIL (which is yellow), the daintily-bobbing DIPPER and the SANDPIPER, a summer visitor which arrives in April to nest by upland streams and lakes.

sandpiper

BEWARE
LOW-FLYING
MOTOR BIKES

Here beginneth
the River Dunsop

O.S. MAP D

SYKES FARM is of great antiquity, for records show that a vaccary(stock) farm had been established here by the 14th.C. Two of the present outbuildings display 17th.C.datestones. In bygone days the house played the dual role of farmhouse and wayside inn.

BRENNAND IS A REMOTE AND LONESOME FARM IN A VAST HOLLOW ENCIRCLED BY BLEAK FELLS. LIKE SYKES IT WAS AN ANCIENT VACCARY, ESTABLISHED IN THIS WILD SETTING BY THE MONKS OF WHALLEY ABBEY, AND IT IS THOUGHT THAT THERE WAS ONCE A CHAPEL HERE. LEAD WAS MINED AT BRENNAND FROM THE MID-17TH.C., THE ORE BEING BROUGHT BY PACKHORSE OVER OUSTER RAKE FOR SMELTING AT A MILL BY SMELT MILL COTTAGES. HAVING PEAKED IN THE MID-19TH.C., THE INDUSTRY FELL INTO DECLINE AND MINING CEASED IN 1873. A RESERVOIR, CONSTRUCTED TO POWER A WATERWHEEL, STANDS ON THE MOOR TO THE N.E. OF THE FARM, AND CAN BE SEEN FROM OUSTER RAKE. BELOW THE FARM, ON THE FAR BANK OF THE RIVER, ARE THE REMAINS OF THE PIT OF ANOTHER WATERWHEEL.

Both the Brennand and the Whitendale are sparkling moorland rivers, and one would expect their confluence to be a picturesque spot. Undoubtedly it was - once - but now, sadly, their union is tortured by masses of waterworks concrete.

9 JUBILEE TOWER 4½ MILES

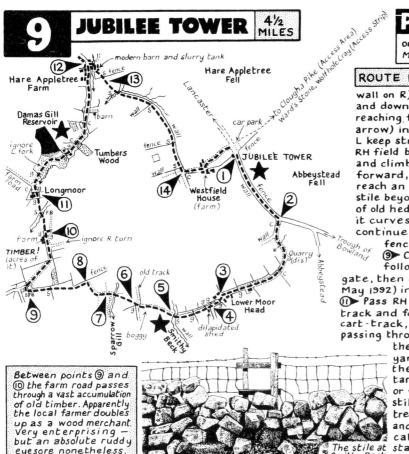

to Clougha Pike (Access Area)
Ward's Stone, Wolfhole Cray (Access Strip)

Hare Appletree Fell

modern barn and slurry tank

(12) s fence (13)

Hare Appletree Farm

Lancaster

Damas Gill Reservoir ★

barn

wall

s

car park

fence

ignore L fork

Tumbers Wood

JUBILEE TOWER ★

Abbeystead Fell

Farm road

Longmoor (11)

fence s

wall

wall

(14) Westfield House (farm)

(10)

ignore R turn

farm

TIMBER! (acres of it)

wall

Trough of Bowland

Quarry (dis)

Abbeystead

(8) fence (6) old track (3)

SFB

(9) (7) (5) (4) Lower Moor Head

Sparrow Gill

★ Smithy Beck

boggy

dilapidated shed

Between points ⑨ and ⑩ the farm road passes through a vast accumulation of old timber. Apparently the local farmer doubles up as a wood merchant. Very enterprising — but an absolute ruddy eyesore nonetheless.

The stile at Smithy Beck

P Jubilee Tower, a square, stone-built, roadside edifice 1¾ miles SE of Quernmore crossroads on the Trough of Bowland road.
Map ref : 542 573

ROUTE DIRECTIONS

① From car park walk SE (with wall on R) along road. ② Turn R (FP sign) over cattle-grid and down farm road. When it forks keep L. ③ Just before reaching farmhouse go L to RH of two gates (wm – blue arrow) into enclosed green track. ④ When track turns L keep straight on (yellow arrow) through gates to follow RH field boundary down to Smithy Beck. ⑤ Ford stream and climb to LH side of remains of old wall. Continue forward, following line of former field boundary, to reach an old metal gate. ⑥ Go ½ L across field to locate stile beyond a tiny stream. ⑦ Forward alongside remains of old hedge. Follow the bank (former field boundary) as it curves R. ⑧ Turn L at crossfence. From fence corner continue forward to pass to L of some Scots pines. Over fence-stile and forward alongside hedge on R. ⑨ Cross stile and footbridge, turn R (FP sign) and follow farm road to farm. ⑩ Pass to L of farm to gate, then descend to footbridge. Cross stile (dated 15 May 1992) in short section of wall then climb to next farm. ⑪ Pass RH end of farm via two gates, forward along cart-track and fork R to gate above trees. Continue along the cart-track, keeping below the reservoir embankment and passing through the grounds of a house, to eventually reach the large farm of Hare Appletree. ⑫ In the farm-yard turn R between buildings down to a gate. Ford the stream, turn R past big modern barn and slurry tank, then bear L up to stiles (choice of two – iron or wood). ⑬ Maintain direction to locate fence-stile (hidden until last minute) 50yds L of line of trees. Forward with fence and stream on L, over stile and forward with wall on L. ⑭ Turn L over cattle-grid and up farm road. (Official right-of-way stays with wall on R, but there's no sign of a path).

Very easy walking in a little-visited area. ⅓ of a mile on a motor-road, 2 miles on farm roads and the rest on pathless pastures which can be muddy. No ladder-stiles. Good views towards the coast.

THE ROOF OF BOWLAND

Jubilee Tower car park is a highly-popular halt for motorists, many of whom do no more than scale the tower steps to admire the view. Of those who pull on their walking boots, 99% will point them eastwards towards the hills, for that is the way to Ward's Stone – at 1841' the highest point in Bowland. A narrow access strip links the Clougha Access Area with the hamlet of Tarnbrook to create a circular route (Jubilee Tower – Ward's Stone – Brown Syke – Tarnbrook – Jubilee Tower) which, being 12½ miles long, cannot be regarded as a 'family walk'. However, a 'there-and-back' trek to Ward's Stone (6½ miles) is feasible on a clear day.

Map showing: Clougha Pike, Grit Fell 1532', Shooters Pile, car park, JUBILEE TOWER, road, lane, Lower Lee, Tarnbrook, Shooter's Crack, Ward's Stone 1841' 1837', Brown Syke, Mallowdale Fell, Wolfhole Crag 1729', Salter's Way, Tarnbrook Wyre

JUBILEE TOWER TO **WARD'S STONE** Path from car park climbs by fence, passing tall cairn (Shooters Pile) as it approaches top of Grit Fell. Just beyond fence-stile a clear path, with marker-poles, drops to depression between Grit Fell and Ward's Stone, where it crosses a shooters' track. Path continues, juicy in places, to first O.S. column, near which is the outcrop called 'Ward's Stone'. About 700yds further on (ENE) is another O.S. column, which is the true summit.

Public access to Wolfhole Crag has recently been negotiated; the route is shown on the new (1996) O.S. Outdoor Leisure map N°41 (Forest of Bowland and Ribblesdale). Those who sally forth into these hills must take O.S. maps and compass, and be generally well-equipped, for this is wild, rough and lonely terrain. NO DOGS ETC., ETC., ETC., ETC., ETC., ETC., ETC., ETC., ETC., ETC., ETC.

THE QUERNMORE BURIAL

In 1973 during the construction of the car park a 7th C. burial of unusual type was brought to light by a mechanical excavator. Only some hair and several finger and toenails remained of the body, but the large woollen shroud in which it had been wrapped was remarkably well-preserved. The coffin which contained them had been made by splitting the trunk of an oak tree and hollowing out each of the two halves into the shape of a boat. Analysis by the radio-carbon process shows that the wood dates from the early 7th C. This burial is particularly interesting as very few of a similar type and date are known, and the shroud is one of the largest pieces of woven cloth from the Dark Ages to be discovered in this country.

The fully conserved remains of the burial are on permanent display in Lancaster City Museum.

JUBILEE TOWER

Jubilee Tower 1887

Built by Hare Appletree resident James Harrison, a rich Liverpool shipbuilder, in 1887 to mark Queen Victoria's Golden Jubilee. Its viewing platform, reached by an external stone staircase, is a superb vantage point from which to survey the entire sweep of Morecambe Bay from Blackpool Tower to the fells of Lakeland.

DAMAS GILL RESERVOIR was built in 1876. It has a capacity of 35 million gallons and supplies water to Lancaster.

O.S. MAP C

P Slaidburn. Car park and toilets at E end of village.
Map ref: 713 523

ROUTE DIRECTIONS

① From car park turn L to follow road over bridge, steeply uphill and round LH bend. ② 60yds above bend take gate (FP sign) on R. Bear slightly R up field and continue to gate/stile in wall at its far end. Forward with wall on L. ③ Immediately past plantation take gate on L to follow other side of wall down to stile. Cross lane and down drive (FP Skelshaw) to Broadhead Farm. ④ Just before bridge turn R and follow way-marks R then L through farmyard to small gate (wm) in wall. Forward with fence on L, and when fence curves away keep straight on to come alongside stream. Pass through gate to walk between fence and stream. ⑤ Just before reaching farm bridge go R through small gate and forward along cart-track. At fork keep R up to house and pass to R of all buildings. ⑥ Turn L down lane. About 100yds past next farm turn R (FP sign) through gate set at angle. Cross field diagonally, aiming towards distant houses of Newton. ⑦ Cross stile and turn ½ R to pass along RH side of line of trees. Cross footbridge (illustrated), follow wall forward to gate and straight on to reach path along L bank of Hodder. After stile curve L across field to gate/stile at bridge. ⑧ Cross bridge and walk up into village to explore its many charms, then return to bridge and turn L through gated stile (FP sign). Forward to small gate (FP sign) then follow river bank. Cross footbridge and stile and forward alongside wall on R. ⑨ Cross gated stile to resume with wall now on your L. At a stile the path enters trees to run along foot of wooded bank, eventually emerging, at a kissing-gate, into a field. ⑩ For alternative riverside finish make for bridge to locate riverside path (wm). Follow waymarks around sewage works (see map) to regain river bank. Otherwise keep straight on along foot of wooded bank then turn L along cart-track. ⑪ Walk R along road to church. ⑫ Go through kissing-gate at rear LH corner of churchyard and follow hedge on L. At hedge-corner continue forward bearing slightly L down to small gate. Turn L to follow riverside path to village green.

concrete and iron footbridge, Easington Brook.

SLAIDBURN
car park and toilets
Whiteholme
plantation
ditch
tarmac lane
Broadhead Farm
Easington Brook
the path here is tightly squeezed between fence and brook, and there are some awkward tree roots to negotiate at one point.
sewage works
Dunnow Hall
Great Dunnow Wood
R. Hodder
site of Manor House
barn
Easington Robinsons Farm
very ancient buildings hereabouts
toilets
NEWTON
Newton Bridge
line of trees and old, sunken track

Bystander at Broadhead

Short, leisurely amble suitable for a hot summer's day. Undulating pastures and riverside meadows - can be very muddy in wet weather. ¾ mile on motor-roads (less if riverside finish is used). No ladder-stiles.

EASINGTON

IS ANCIENT ENOUGH TO HAVE BEEN RECORDED (AS 'ESINTUNE') IN THE DOMESDAY SURVEY OF 1086. IT WAS THEN (AND STILL IS) BUT A TINY HAMLET COMPRISING TWO FARMS AND ASSOCIATED BUILDINGS. A MANOR HOUSE WAS BUILT HERE IN THE MID-16TH C BUT, BEING CLOSE TO THE BROOK, WAS SUSCEPTIBLE TO FLOODING AND WAS ABANDONED c1700. NOTE THE DATESTONE 1699 OVER THE DOOR AT ROBINSONS FARM.

NEWTON

, or Newton-in-Bowland to give it its Sunday name, should definitely not be missed, for this lovely, mellow, olde-worlde hotch-potch of a village has more than its fair share of noteworthy 17th-19th C. buildings.

Parkers Arms

Approaching from the graceful Newton Bridge you will first be confronted by The Hall, a fine Georgian residence. Should you have taken the author's advice to sally forth on a hot summer's day you will then no doubt joyfully dive into the splendid Parkers Arms (also Georgian) for a much-needed noggin. In the centre of the village is Salisbury Cottage (formerly Newton Old Hall), whilst at the W end of the main street stands John Brabbin's Old School House (JMB 1757). Up the lane to its left is the Friends Meeting House (1767) and, a few yards beyond and across the road, a Quaker burial ground. A local Quaker and Liberal politician – John Bright (1811-89) – was a prominent reformer who was influential in the Repeal of the Corn Laws.

SLAIDBURN PARISH CHURCH

This imposing building is dedicated to St. Andrew and dates back to at least the 12th C. The 15th C. TOWER is the oldest part of the present church, the interior of which has changed little since the early 18th C. There is a Norman FONT (c1229) with an Elizabethan oak cover, and old BOX PEWS dated 1616-1749. The magnificent Jacobean ROOD SCREEN, between the nave and chancel, was erected in 1634, and the Georgian three-decker PULPIT was installed in 1740. Note also the curious CELTIC HEAD high on the north wall of the nave, and the SHOOTING-STAR in the Nativity scene of the EAST WINDOW. In the CHURCHYARD is a SUNDIAL (illustrated) dated 1796, and, near the tower, part of the shaft of a MEDIEVAL CROSS.

–•–•–

Adjacent to the church is the OLD GRAMMAR SCHOOL, founded by John Brennand in 1717 and still in use as the village school. CHURCH STILE FARM, opposite the church, is on the site of the old village inn. (The church was once the centre of the village).

–•–•–

DUNNOW HALL

now stands empty and forlorn, its aura of gloom reflecting the sadness in its history. It was built by a young man in the 1830s as a home for his bride-to-be but, tragically, the girl died and never enjoyed the mansion's charms.

FOR NOTES ON SLAIDBURN SEE WALK 19
FOR NOTES ON THE RIVER HODDER SEE WALK 23

O.S. MAP D

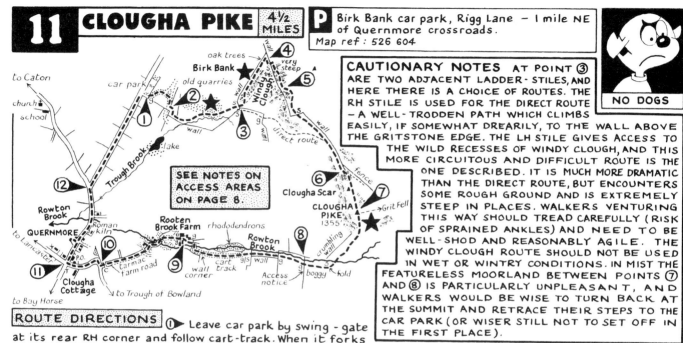

11 CLOUGHA PIKE — 4½ MILES

P Birk Bank car park, Rigg Lane — 1 mile NE of Quernmore crossroads.
Map ref: 526 604

NO DOGS

CAUTIONARY NOTES AT POINT ③ ARE TWO ADJACENT LADDER-STILES, AND HERE THERE IS A CHOICE OF ROUTES. THE RH STILE IS USED FOR THE DIRECT ROUTE — A WELL-TRODDEN PATH WHICH CLIMBS EASILY, IF SOMEWHAT DREARILY, TO THE WALL ABOVE THE GRITSTONE EDGE. THE LH STILE GIVES ACCESS TO THE WILD RECESSES OF WINDY CLOUGH, AND THIS MORE CIRCUITOUS AND DIFFICULT ROUTE IS THE ONE DESCRIBED. IT IS MUCH MORE DRAMATIC THAN THE DIRECT ROUTE, BUT ENCOUNTERS SOME ROUGH GROUND AND IS EXTREMELY STEEP IN PLACES. WALKERS VENTURING THIS WAY SHOULD TREAD CAREFULLY (RISK OF SPRAINED ANKLES) AND NEED TO BE WELL-SHOD AND REASONABLY AGILE. THE WINDY CLOUGH ROUTE SHOULD NOT BE USED IN WET OR WINTRY CONDITIONS. IN MIST THE FEATURELESS MOORLAND BETWEEN POINTS ⑦ AND ⑧ IS PARTICULARLY UNPLEASANT, AND WALKERS WOULD BE WISE TO TURN BACK AT THE SUMMIT AND RETRACE THEIR STEPS TO THE CAR PARK (OR WISER STILL NOT TO SET OFF IN THE FIRST PLACE).

ROUTE DIRECTIONS ① Leave car park by swing-gate at its rear RH corner and follow cart-track. When it forks go R, then R again along cross path. ② Don't use gate (private) but turn L along duckboards to clear, rising path, with wall on R. Keep to LH side of stream, then climb to two adjacent ladder-stiles. ③ See 'CAUTIONARY NOTES'. For Windy Clough route take LH stile. Forward along thin path to L of valley, and in 30yds fork L up rising path. It soon peters out, but continue to slant up the hillside (with care) to reach ridge-wall. Follow it forward (thin path). ④ At wall-corner path(!) descends R to ladder-stile. Cross it and turn R to climb very steeply by wall. ⑤ A very rough, rocky depression may be avoided by making a wide-ish detour to the L. Cross ladder-stile and bear L to follow wall on L. ⑥ When wall ends climb over gritstone blocks but don't follow fence. Clear path 30yds from edge heads for cairn on skyline, then straight on to summit. ⑦ Straight on from summit (almost due S) to locate slightly sunken path descending and swinging R to run parallel with a crumbling wall. Thin, but obvious (in clear weather) path crosses tiny stream then runs down parallel with it to reach

Strenuous. Climb of about 1030' from car park to summit – very beautiful and with superb views, but rough underfoot and extremely steep in places (see 'CAUTIONARY NOTES'). Descent easy, though some boggy patches may be encountered around the headwaters of Rowton Brook. Last mile is on motor-roads. 3 ladder-stiles. Not recommended in mist.

gate and Access notice. ⑧➤ Straight on across field to take RH of two gates, forward with wall on L to gate/stile, then follow cart-track down to farm. ⑨➤ Straight through farmyard and out along its access road. ⑩➤ Turn R down road. ⑪➤ At crossroads turn R (Caton) along Rigg Lane. ⑫➤ Turn R at road-junction.

CLOUGHA PIKE
Pronounced 'Cloffa'

Bilberry

is not the highest fell in Bowland, but it is certainly one of the best-known and most-visited. It is a rough and rocky hill ; a wild place of heather and bilberry, tumbled boulders and grey, splintered gritstone crags. The old and extensive quarries near the start of our walk at Birk Bank once produced Clougha slate for roofing.

From the O.S. column and wind-shelters at Clougha's rugged summit – one of the few in the district with public access – there is the most stunning view across Lancashire's coastal plains to the Lune estuary and the shimmering waters of Morecambe Bay, backed by the shapely Lakeland skyline. Blackpool Tower is visible, and particularly prominent are a massive square box and a green dome – the former being the nuclear power station at Heysham and the latter the Ashton Memorial at Lancaster.

QUERNMORE
Pronounced 'Kworma'

is so named from the querns, or millstones, which were once produced hereabouts from local stone. A straggling, sprawling village, it rather lacks character and has no real focal point.

In the 18th C the remains of two ROMAN POTTERY KILNS were found in the area, and one of the sites is passed on our walk. It may be seen at the corner of a small roadside copse about 300 yards beyond the crossroads at point ⑪. The kilns contained remnants of pottery, tiles and bricks from the 3rd century AD.

The handsome CHURCH OF ST. PETER stands in splendid isolation a good distance to the N of the village, and to include it in our walk would necessitate an extra mile of road-walking – probably only to find its doors locked. A better idea would be to drive along later. Though its architecture is 14th C-style it was built in 1860. The stained glass of the E window – made in Lancaster but for export to France – was salvaged from the wreck of the 'Fairy Vision', which ran aground in fog near the Rhône estuary.

Quernmore Church

The stile at the head of Windy Clough (badly in need of repair – 25-7-06)

ROOTEN BROOK FARM (datestone 1693) and ROWTON BROOK FARM stand within 200 yards of each other, which must cause no end of confusion. In the 18th C the Rowton Brook area had a thriving hat-making industry.

O.S. MAPS | A | C

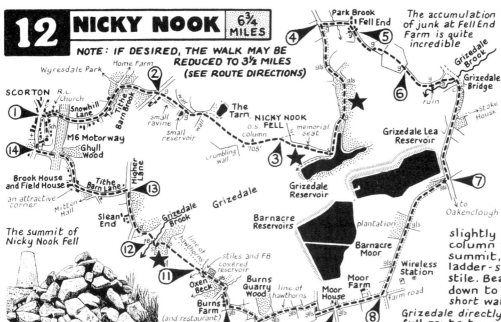

12 NICKY NOOK 6¾ MILES

NOTE: IF DESIRED, THE WALK MAY BE REDUCED TO 3½ MILES (SEE ROUTE DIRECTIONS)

The accumulation of junk at Fell End Farm is quite incredible

ROUTE DIRECTIONS

① From village centre walk up Snowhill (Lane). It crosses M6, swings L then R over stream and climbs steeply. ② At T-junction take facing kissing-gate and climb obvious path straight up hillside. After passing through a gap in a wall the path bears slightly R and heads for summit (O.S. column visible). Straight on (68°) from summit, following clear path towards ladder-stile. ③ Don't cross ladder-stile. Bear R to follow wall steeply down to stile onto gravel track. For short walk turn R and follow track down Grizedale directly to footbridge at point ⑫. For full route turn L. Track goes through gate into woodland, then continues through open pastures. ④ Turn R (BW sign) down farm road. Turn R at farmhouse to follow BW signs to iron gate. ⑤ Up stony track alongside fence on L. Go L through small iron gate (wm) then turn R to go up through gateway (wm) in fence and straight across next field to gate (wm). ⑥ Forward alongside ruined wall on L. Through two gates then bear R to bridge. Turn R up road. ⑦ Just past Waterworks entrance turn R (FP sign) through gate/stile and up cart-track. ⑧ At 'crossroads' just past wireless station turn R down farm road. ⑨ At Moor House go straight on along an enclosed green track. It turns sharp R then sharp L (wm) and continues as a green track, eventually turning R to descend to farm. ⑩ Turn R and pass to R of all farm buildings, then R at T-junction and L along track to covered reservoir. Straight ahead to cross small ravine via stiles and footbridge. ⑪ Bear slightly L across big field to locate stile into wood at its bottom RH corner. Descend very steeply to footbridge. ⑫ Straight forward (SP Higher Lane), keeping just below edge of

Climb, steep in places, of 475' from Tithe Barn Brook to summit of Nicky Nook, followed by steep, rough descent to Grizedale Reservoir. Another steep, slippery descent to footbridge at point ⑫. Mostly on good tracks and paths, with 1¾ miles on quiet motor-roads. No ladder-stiles. Best done when rhododendrons are in bloom.

12

wood, then continue forward up tarmac lane. ⑬► Turn L at junction to follow lane down and under motorway. ⑭► Turn R at T-junction and in a few yards take gate on R and climb to church. Leave by lych-gate to follow lane past school and L down to village centre.

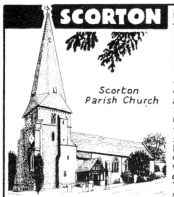

Scorton Parish Church

SCORTON

is a picturesque village of cobble-fringed, picture-postcard cottages. It was a peaceful village, too, until 1963; then the M6 came slicing through the landscape, missing Scorton by a hair's breadth, and the villagers had to learn to live with the constant drone of traffic. There are two fine churches. The R.C.Church (St.Mary and St.James), which is passed at the beginning of the walk, was built in 1861. The Parish Church of St.Peter was designed by the Lancaster architects Daley and Austin, and built at a cost of £13,000. Upon its completion a consecration service was led by the Bishop of Manchester on the eve of St.Peter's Day, 1879. The elegant spire – made of cedar shingles – is 150 feet high and is topped by a weathervane depicting the crossed keys of St. Peter. The clock faces are approximately 5 feet wide. Notable features of the equally splendid interior are the beautifully painted ceiling, the oak pews – each carved with a different design – and the lovely E. window showing St. Peter in the centre and the Transfiguration of Christ above.

NICKY NOOK FELL

is Bowland's most westerly vantage point and, though of modest height, provides marvellous views – particularly across Lancashire's coastal plain to Morecambe Bay and the Lakeland Fells beyond. GRIZEDALE ('valley of wild pigs') is supremely beautiful, and the wooded setting of GRIZEDALE RESERVOIR (constructed 1861-3) is one of the prettiest scenes you will encounter in this series of walks. The other reservoirs – GRIZEDALE LEA and BARNACRE – present a totally contrasting scenario, their harsh severity appearing completely alien to the surrounding landscape.

THE TARN

Great Crested Grebe

IS A DESOLATE, REEDY POOL WITH A FEW TORTURED-LOOKING SCOTS PINES AT ITS WESTERN END. THOUGH VISUALLY DISAPPOINTING, IT PROVIDES AN ATTRACTIVE HABITAT FOR MANY SPECIES OF WATERFOWL, AND BIRD-WATCHERS' HIDES OF UNUSUAL CONSTRUCTION LINE ITS SHORES.

O.S.MAP **E**

13 THE GREAT STONE OF FOURSTONES | 5 MILES

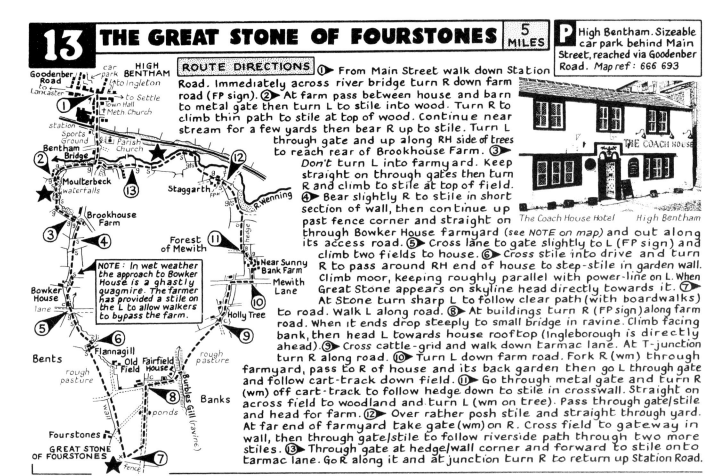

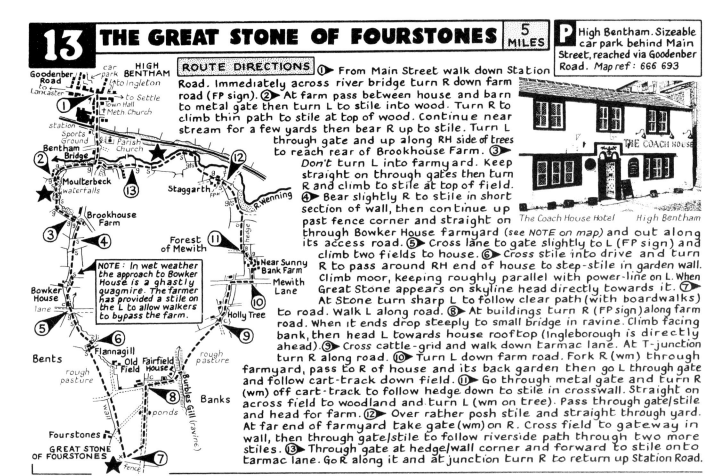
P High Bentham. Sizeable car park behind Main Street, reached via Goodenber Road. Map ref: 666 693

The Coach House Hotel   High Bentham

ROUTE DIRECTIONS

① From Main Street walk down Station Road. Immediately across river bridge turn R down farm road (FP sign). **②** At farm pass between house and barn to metal gate then turn L to stile into wood. Turn R to climb thin path to stile at top of wood. Continue near stream for a few yards then bear R up to stile. Turn L through gate and up along RH side of trees to reach rear of Brookhouse Farm. **③** *Don't turn L into farmyard.* Keep straight on through gates then turn R and climb to stile at top of field. **④** Bear slightly R to stile in short section of wall, then continue up past fence corner and straight on through Bowker House farmyard (*see NOTE on map*) and out along its access road. **⑤** Cross lane slightly to L (FP sign) and climb two fields to house. **⑥** Cross stile into drive and turn R to pass around RH end of house to step-stile in garden wall. Climb moor, keeping roughly parallel with power-line on L. When Great Stone appears on skyline head directly towards it. **⑦** At Stone turn sharp L to follow clear path (with boardwalks) to road. Walk L along road. **⑧** At buildings turn R (FP sign) along farm road. When it ends drop steeply to small bridge in ravine. Climb facing bank, then head L towards house rooftop (Ingleborough is directly ahead). **⑨** Cross cattle-grid and walk down tarmac lane. At T-junction turn R along road. **⑩** Turn L down farm road. Fork R (wm) through farmyard, pass to R of house and its back garden then go L through gate and follow cart-track down field. **⑪** Go through metal gate and turn R (wm) off cart-track to follow hedge down to stile in crosswall. Straight on across field to woodland and turn L (wm on tree). Pass through gate/stile and head for farm. **⑫** Over rather posh stile and straight through yard. At far end of farmyard take gate (wm) on R. Cross field to gateway in wall, then through gate/stile to follow riverside path through two more stiles. **⑬** Through gate at hedge/wall corner and forward to stile onto tarmac lane. Go R along it and at junction turn R to return up Station Road.

NOTE: In wet weather the approach to Bowker House is a ghastly quagmire. The farmer has provided a stile on the L to allow walkers to bypass the farm.

(Map labels:) car park, HIGH BENTHAM, Goodenber Road to Lancaster, to Ingleton, to Settle, Town Hall, Meth. Church, station, Sports Ground, Parish Church, Bentham Bridge, Moulterbeck waterfalls, Staggarth, R. Wenning, Brookhouse Farm, Forest of Mewith, Near Sunny Bank Farm, Mewith Lane, Bowker House lane, Holly Tree, Flannagill, Old Fairfield Field House, Bents, rough pasture, Banks, ponds, Burbles Gill (ravine), Fourstones, GREAT STONE OF FOURSTONES, wall, fence

Easy walking with no steep gradients. ¾ mile on motor roads, mostly with either pavements or unenclosed grass verges. I mile over rough moorland pasture, where a compass would be useful in mist. No ladder-stiles.

Mail Box,
Flannagill

THE RIVER WENNING TAKES ITS NAME FROM THE OLD ENGLISH 'WAN', MEANING 'THE DARK ONE'. IT IS BORN NEAR CLAPHAM, WHERE STREAMS EMERGING FROM THE CAVES OF INGLEBOROUGH CONVERGE UPON THOSE RUSHING DOWN THE N.E. SLOPES OF BOWLAND. SWOLLEN NEAR HORNBY BY THE HINDBURN, ITS MAJOR TRIBUTARY, THE WENNING THEN FLOWS SEDATELY ON FOR A FURTHER 1¼ MILES TO ENTER THE LUNE EN ROUTE FOR LANCASTER AND MORECAMBE BAY.

BENTHAM has a documented history going back to the time of the Domesday Book (1086). The name is from the Old English 'beonet ham' (homestead in the open grassland). By 1302 there were two separate settlements of High and Low Bentham, and there are a number of 17th C. houses in and around High Bentham's main street. HIGH MILL (the large mill

we pass by the River Wenning) was built in 1750 for the spinning of flax. It later manufactured cotton cloth, and in 1931 was purchased by Wenning Silks, which closed c 1960. The RAILWAY arrived in 1850, and the TOWN HALL was built 27 years later. The AUCTION MART (still trading) was established in 1903 and the METHODIST CHURCH in Station Road dates from 1905. Wednesday is MARKET DAY in Bentham, and Thursday is half-day closing. ● The Victorian Gothic-style PARISH CHURCH (St. Margaret of Antioch) stands on a small hill overlooking the river. It was founded by HORNBY ROUGHSEDGE, owner of High Mill, whose 10-year-old daughter Margaret laid the foundation stone on 30 June 1836. The ROUGHSEDGE MEMORIAL can be seen on the N. wall of the chancel. The church was extended in 1901, when some exceptionally lovely STAINED-GLASS WINDOWS were installed. Admire also the beautiful applique hanging of the Holy Family.

THE GREAT STONE OF FOURSTONES, known locally simply as 'The Big Stone', stands on the Yorkshire/Lancashire boundary. It is a massive boulder termed by geologists as an 'erratic', ie a stray rock foreign to the surrounding strata, and was probably deposited by a melting glacier at the end of the Ice Age. Originally, as the name suggests, there were three other stones which, so legend has it, were snaffled by the Devil for building his bridge at Kirkby Lonsdale. More probably they were broken up by farmers for grindstones or walling material. The most remarkable feature of the 12' high stone is the flight of steps (easier to get up than down) which has been hewn into its side. This is a magnificent viewpoint.

FAIRFIELD HOUSE is a beautifully maintained property. ● The farmyard at STAGGARTH is a delightfully mellow and old-fashioned place.

O.S. MAP B

14 WHITEWELL & BROWSHOLME 6¾ MILES

ROUTE DIRECTIONS

①► Walk up road past black and white Village Hall, turn R up steps (FP sign) and climb field to house. ②► Pass between house and old waterworks tunnel and climb steeply (no path) to stile in crosswall. Keep on up with wall on R. ③► Through iron kissing-gate, then another, and follow wall on L. ④► Straight down farmyard, turn R at bottom and, in a few yards, L (wm) and forward with wall on L to stile in crosswall. ⑤► Straight on down field to gate/stile in crossfence, then bear R to reach track leading to farm. ⑥► Pass house, go through gate on L, then resume original direction, gradually descending to small stream on L. Cross it, re-cross it almost immediately, cross fence-stile and turn L to follow stream down. Cross it again at footbridge and climb field to gate/stile. ⑦► Turn L along lane then R across cattle-grid to follow farm road to Lees House Farm. ⑧► Pass blue tank, go L through gate and pass behind house to stile into wood. Thin path soon descends steeply to stream. Cross footbridge. ⑨► Turn R in field and follow stream. Cross stile in fence then turn L and climb steeply to gate/stile in crossfence. Straight ahead past barn and up cart-track. ⑩► Where track bends L right-of-way goes straight on up field and passes in front of house, but farmer would probably prefer you to stay with cart-track and follow it round into farmyard. Pass between buildings and turn L along access road. ⑪► Where road begins to curve R go through gate on L and cross field towards house in trees. Through gate and walk L up road. ⑫► Go up Browsholme Hall car park access road and in 30yds turn L through gate and up cart-track. ⑬► Cross cattle-grid, go through gate and climb field to pass RH end of

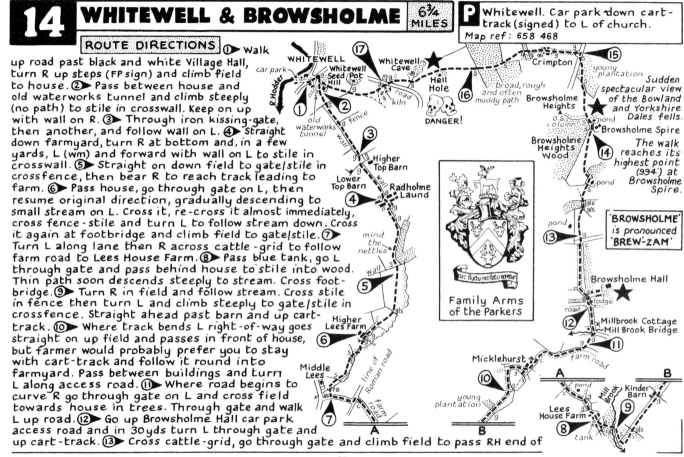

Family Arms of the Parkers

'BROWSHOLME' is pronounced 'BREW-ZAM'

Sudden spectacular view of the Bowland and Yorkshire Dales fells

The walk reaches its highest point (994') at Browsholme Spire.

mind the nettles

DANGER!

Fairly strenuous undulating walk with 3 steep gradients (2 up, 1 down). Mostly on farm tracks and pathless pastures. ½ mile on quiet motor-roads. 1 ladder-stile. Because of livestock, dogs will need to be on lead most of the time.

wood. When church-like building comes into view aim slightly to R of it. Cross stile, pass pond, then L over stile between gateposts and climb to 'church'. **14▶** Follow path (FP sign) at edge of wood, cross access road and straight down field to stile into plantation. Descend to roadside stile. **15▶** Along farm road to Crimpton. Go straight through yard and follow fence on L. Through two small gates (wm) and on to stile at inner corner of plantation. Forward along forest track to stile. **16▶** Straight down field towards trees to locate ladder-stile. Descend to roadside gate. **17▶** Cross road to kiln. Ascend broad green path, soon forking R along hillside to gate in wall. Descend to RH side of house to rejoin outward route.

WHITEWELL

This tiny village is far-famed for its idyllic setting. Here the Hodder rushes through a wooded gorge of such beauty as to have earned the nickname 'Little Switzerland.' The INN AT WHITEWELL – a splendid country hotel – was formerly the Manor

Village Hall. The walk starts up the road past this building.

House and has parts over 500 years old. The adjacent PARISH CHURCH OF ST. MICHAEL (1818) occupies the site of a much older chapel (c1400) and has a fine Jacobean pulpit.

Of the 3 CAVES/POTHOLES shown on the map, HELL HOLE and WHITEWELL CAVE may be conveniently visited. HELL HOLE, in a clump of trees, is a DANGEROUS open shaft 45' deep. To locate WHITEWELL CAVE detour down to the R immediately after crossing the ladder-stile. A tiny stream sinks near the cave entrance at the base of a prominent scar. The small entrance leads to a larger sloping passage with the stream coming in from the R.

Hell Hole

BROWSHOLME HALL

This superb Jacobean mansion is the ancestral home of the Parkers, who have lived here since 1507. The house contains fine oak carvings, period furniture, arms and armour, textiles, rare books, stained glass and a collection of antiquities ranging from Stone Age axes to a fragment of a zeppelin. One relic which you won't see, however, is the human skull which is kept in a locked cupboard; legend has it that disaster will strike if it is seen by anyone other than members of the family.

BROWSHOLME SPIRE was built to act as a landmark to shooters on the fells. The castellated wall originally had a central archway.

● DURING THE 14TH AND 15TH CENTURIES RADHOLME LAUND (THEN A WOODEN LODGE) SERVED AS THE ADMINISTRATIVE HQ OF A HUGE DEER PARK. ● LEES HOUSE IS A JACOBEAN FARMHOUSE WITH FINE MULLIONED WINDOWS AND A DOORHEAD DATED 1678. ● CRIMPTON IS KNOWN LOCALLY AS 'OUR LADY OF THE FELLS'.

O.S. MAP | F

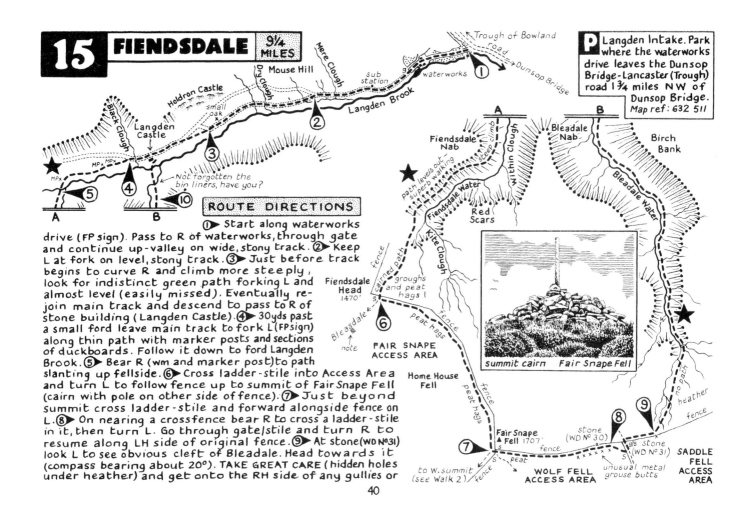

15 FIENDSDALE 9¼ MILES

P Langden Intake. Park where the waterworks drive leaves the Dunsop Bridge-Lancaster (Trough) road 1¾ miles NW of Dunsop Bridge. Map ref: 632 511

Trough of Bowland road → Dunsop Bridge

Mere Clough

Mouse Hill

Dry Clough

sub station

waterworks ①

Langden Brook

Holdron Castle

small oak

②

Black Clough

Langden Castle

③

Not forgotten the bin liners, have you?

MP× MP× MP

★

MP×

⑤ ④ ⑩

A   B

A   B

Fiendsdale Nab

steep climb

Within Clough

Bleadale Nab

Birch Bank

path levels out—superb walking

Fiendsdale Water

Red Scars

Bleadale Water

★

cairned path

Kite Clough

groughs and peat hags !

Fiendsdale Head 1470'

Bleadale note

fence

⑥

fence

peat hags

FAIR SNAPE ACCESS AREA

summit cairn   Fair Snape Fell

★

no path

heather

fence

Home House Fell

peat hags

fence

⑨

Fair Snape Fell 1707'

fence

to W. summit (see Walk 2)

⑦

peat

fence

stone (WD Nº 30)

⑧

u/s stone (WD Nº 31)

SADDLE FELL ACCESS AREA

WOLF FELL ACCESS AREA

unusual metal grouse butts

ROUTE DIRECTIONS

① Start along waterworks drive (FP sign). Pass to R of waterworks, through gate and continue up-valley on wide, stony track. ② Keep L at fork on level, stony track. ③ Just before track begins to curve R and climb more steeply, look for indistinct green path forking L and almost level (easily missed). Eventually re-join main track and descend to pass to R of stone building (Langden Castle). ④ 30yds past a small ford leave main track to fork L (FP sign) along thin path with marker posts and sections of duckboards. Follow it down to ford Langden Brook. ⑤ Bear R (wm and marker post) to path slanting up fellside. ⑥ Cross ladder-stile into Access Area and turn L to follow fence up to summit of Fair Snape Fell (cairn with pole on other side of fence). ⑦ Just beyond summit cross ladder-stile and forward alongside fence on L. ⑧ On nearing a crossfence bear R to cross a ladder-stile in it, then turn L. Go through gate/stile and turn R to resume along LH side of original fence. ⑨ At stone (WD Nº 31) look L to see obvious cleft of Bleadale. Head towards it (compass bearing about 20°). TAKE GREAT CARE (hidden holes under heather) and get onto the RH side of any gullies or

Strenuous. Climb (steep and loose initially) of 900' from Langden Brook (Point ⑤) to summit of Fair Snape Fell. Bogs and peat hags on the highest ground. Clear paths apart from one very awkward ½-mile stretch of deep heather. No motor-roads. 3 ladder-stiles (all within Access Area, so dogs won't be crossing them anyway). Magnificent ravine scenery. Vertigo sufferers may be unhappy in upper Bleadale.

IMPORTANT NOTES – TO BE READ BEFORE LEAVING HOME

This is taking a 'family' walk to its limit. The full circuit is a rough, tough expedition FOR EXPERIENCED AND WELL-EQUIPPED WALKERS ONLY. It is certainly not suitable for young children, should not be attempted in mist, and is out of the question in wintry conditions. The fording of Langden Brook and Bleadale Water may cause problems after heavy rain, and the author's tip is to pop a couple of plastic bin-liners into your rucksack. Dogs may be taken only as far as the fence at Fiendsdale Head, but this would make an excellent 'there and back' walk (6¾ miles). To the summit of Fair Snape Fell and return is 9 miles, but the climb by the fence from Fiendsdale Head is a long, weary drag. If you're not doing the full circuit it's scarcely worth the effort (unless you're an inveterate summit-bagger). Those intending to walk the full circular route should note the following : –

- The path down Bleadale is permissive, and the landowners (N.W. Water) request that walkers avoid the valley during the bird-nesting season (mid-April to the end of July). There may also be shooting or fire restrictions (see Access Areas P8). For up-to-date information ring Mr. Peter Guy, N.W. Water, Preston (01772 822200).
- Allow plenty of time – the descent of Bleadale will take longer than you think.

watercourses. Head for RH side of main valley, where a thin path develops high above the stream. Follow it WITH CARE down the valley. ⑩ On nearing Langden Castle make a beeline for it, fording first Bleadale Water then Langden Brook. Turn R at Langden Castle to retrace outward route.

The tree-lined drive makes an attractive start to the walk, but beyond the waterworks the Langden Valley initially looks somewhat unpromising. The broad flood-plain strewn with boulders is an indication of the potential force, in storm conditions, of the normally innocuous-looking brook. Two 'castles' are passed on the way up the valley, but neither is really a castle at all. HOLDRON CASTLE is a group of natural rock pinnacles high on the hillside to the R. LANGDEN CASTLE is merely a stone hut with a tin roof. Its age is uncertain, but the gothic shape of its doorway and windows suggests that it could have been a 19th C shooting-lodge. Beyond Langden Castle the scenery improves dramatically as the valley narrows between towering, heather- and bracken-clothed slopes. This is where things get really exciting!

Langden Castle

BLEADALE IS THE WILDEST AND MOST THRILLING PLACE IN THIS BOOK. IT IS A 'SENSITIVE' AREA IN THAT IT IS A BREEDING-GROUND FOR SOME QUITE RARE BIRDS.

O.S. MAPS C* D E F

* tiny section only

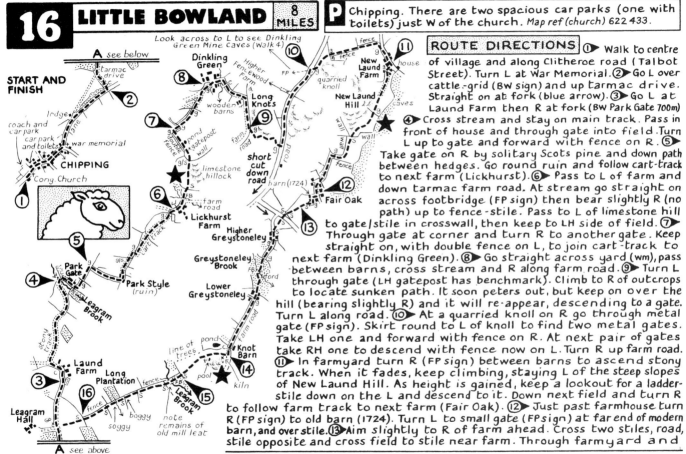

16 LITTLE BOWLAND — 8 MILES

P Chipping. There are two spacious car parks (one with toilets) just W of the church. Map ref (church) 622 433.

ROUTE DIRECTIONS

① Walk to centre of village and along Clitheroe road (Talbot Street). Turn L at War Memorial. ② Go L over cattle-grid (BW sign) and up tarmac drive. Straight on at fork (blue arrow). ③ Go L at Laund Farm then R at fork (BW Park Gate 700m) ④ Cross stream and stay on main track. Pass in front of house and through gate into field. Turn L up to gate and forward with fence on R. ⑤ Take gate on R by solitary Scots pine and down path between hedges. Go round ruin and follow cart-track to next farm (Lickhurst). ⑥ Pass to L of farm and down tarmac farm road. At stream go straight on across footbridge (FP sign) then bear slightly R (no path) up to fence-stile. Pass to L of limestone hill to gate/stile in crosswall, then keep to LH side of field. ⑦ Through gate at corner and turn R to another gate. Keep straight on, with double fence on L, to join cart-track to next farm (Dinkling Green). ⑧ Go straight across yard (wm), pass between barns, cross stream and R along farm road. ⑨ Turn L through gate (LH gatepost has benchmark). Climb to R of outcrops to locate sunken path. It soon peters out, but keep on over the hill (bearing slightly R) and it will re-appear, descending to a gate. Turn L along road. ⑩ At a quarried knoll on R go through metal gate (FP sign). Skirt round to L of knoll to find two metal gates. Take LH one and forward with fence on R. At next pair of gates take RH one to descend with fence now on L. Turn R up farm road. ⑪ In farmyard turn R (FP sign) between barns to ascend stony track. When it fades, keep climbing, staying L of the steep slopes of New Laund Hill. As height is gained, keep a lookout for a ladder-stile down on the L and descend to it. Down next field and turn R to follow farm track to next farm (Fair Oak). ⑫ Just past farmhouse turn R (FP sign) to old barn (1724). Turn L to small gate (FP sign) at far end of modern barn, and over stile. ⑬ Aim slightly to R of farm ahead. Cross two stiles, road, stile opposite and cross field to stile near farm. Through farmyard and

Map labels

Look across to L to see Dinkling Green Mine Caves (Walk 4)

A see below

START AND FINISH

Dinkling Green

Higher Fencewood Farm

New Laund Farm

house

fence

quarried knoll

New Laund Hill

caves

tarmac drive

lane

lrdge

coach and car park

car park and toilets

war memorial

CHIPPING

Cong. Church

Long Knots

wooden barns

double fence

pond gatepost wall

gls

limestone hillock

short cut down road

barn (1724)

Fair Oak

wall

FB

farm road

Lickhurst Farm

Higher Greystoneley

Greystoneley Brook

ford

FB

Lower Greystoneley

farm road

Park Gate

Park Style (ruin)

gls

cart track

stony track

Leagram Brook

line of trees

pond

Knot Barn

pool

kiln

Laund Farm

Long Plantation

fence

Leagram Brook

Leagram Hall

GB

fence

boggy

soggy

note remains of old mill leat

A see above

42

An undulating walk largely on lanes and farm roads/tracks. Easy going – gentle gradients – and good underfoot. 1½ miles on motor-roads. 1 ladder-stile. Many of the fields are likely to contain livestock. Fine views of Pendle, the upper Hodder Valley and the Hodder gorge. The SHORT CUT shown on the map reduces the walk to 6¾ miles and avoids the sole ladder-stile and the most strenuous section (the climb around New Laund Hill).

along farm road. ⑭▶ Cross cattle-grid by barn and turn R up green path. Pass to R of kiln and quarry, then bear very slightly L (no path) across field to fence-stile (wm). ⑮▶ Descend thin path to footbridge, then rise to stile in crossfence. Keep straight on alongside fence on R. ⑯▶ When fence on R ends, go straight across field. Turn L down drive to re-trace outward route to Chipping.

CHIPPING

, which dates back to Saxon times, is picturesque and full of charm. The haphazard clusters of ancient stone cottages, sturdy church and cosy inns make this a truly quintessential English village. The name means 'market', and whilst several English towns and villages incorporate the name with another one (e.g. Chipping Sodbury, Chipping Norton), this is the only instance of 'Chipping' on its own. The 17th C school and almshouses were endowed by John Brabin, a wealthy cloth merchant. The splendid St. Bartholomew's Church is of uncertain vintage, having been rebuilt in 1506 and 1873, but it is known from records that a church existed in Chipping in 1230. The only remaining relic from the 13th C building is the piscina (stone basin for rinsing chalice) in the chancel. The unusual dormer window was installed c 1450 and was so positioned that its light would fall on the Rood (Crucifix). In the Middle Ages there were at least five water-mills sited along Chipping Beck.

Tillotsons Arms

● LAUND FARM claims to be the 'Home of the Blue-Faced Leicester', but this breed of sheep originates from Hexham.
● DINKLING GREEN is a cluster of 17th and 18th C buildings in a delightful setting.
● NEW LAUND – also in a beautiful setting – was once a forest-keeper's house.

LITTLE BOWLAND

is the name given to the triangle of country bordered on the east by the Hodder and on the north and west by the high fells from Totridge to Fair Snape. With its short, springy turf, limestone knolls and scattered woodlands it is a beautiful walking area.

LEAGRAM HALL AND THE DEER PARKS

During the 13th C the felling of trees and the establishment of cattle farms conflicted with the use of the area as a hunting ground, and, in order to conserve the deer, two huge launds, or deer parks, were created at Radholme (see Walk 14) and Chipping. These parks were enclosed by a bank surmounted by oak palings and thorns, and an 8' wide by 4' deep ditch. These parks were obsolete by the 16th C, but traces of the ramparts can still be seen along this walk. Surrounded by beautiful parkland, LEAGRAM HALL occupies the site of a former lodge which was the HQ of Chipping Laund. During the 16th C the Hall was a refuge for Catholic priests, who in those days were persecuted.

Just beyond New Laund Farm are 3 caves known as FAIRY HOLES, in which have been discovered animal bones – pounded to extract the marrow – and various Bronze Age domestic utensils. There is, unfortunately, no right-of-way to the caves.

The lonesome pine at point ⑤

O.S. MAP F

43

17 CROSS OF GREET BRIDGE — 6 MILES

ROUTE DIRECTIONS

① Cross cattle-grid and walk down road. In 100yds turn R (FP sign) to gate in wall and follow clear path down moor to eventually reach gate in wall-corner near a small ruin. **②** From gate go forward 25yds then turn R (compass bearing 260°) along faint path. Look down to your L to see a prominent raised bank running away to a wall-gate. **③** When in line with this bank turn L and descend (no path) towards it. Cross tiny stream (* *note that later in the day you will return to this spot – with a bit of luck and a favouring wind*) and follow bank to gate/stile (there is a thin path to the R of the bank). **④** Head towards building in trees, en route joining a farm track. **⑤** 50yds past barn take gate/stile on R. Go forward past the end of a walled green lane and alongside wall on L to gate/stile. Turn L down to stepping-stones then straight on up towards ruins. **⑥** Pass through gap in wall between the two ruins, then turn R to climb alongside the wooded clough. Cross a small wooded tributary to a stile, then continue up hill to turn R along farm track. **⑦** Walk R along road, and immediately beyond trees on L go L over stile. Bear R up to gate/stile at top of field, then follow fence on L up to farm. **⑧** Turn L through gate at farm road, then in a few paces R towards barn. Use gate/stile to pass to L of barn and forward alongside wall on R to gate/stile. **⑨** Straight on (no path), aiming to RH end of conifers, then follow plantation wall down to road. Walk L down road to Cross of Greet Bridge. **⑩** At far side of bridge turn R to descend faint path alongside wall. Keep L of big sheepfold to gate and continue down thin riverside path. **⑪** Clear path leaves river and heads towards farm. Cross tributary stream near its confluence to an old green cart-track slanting L up hillside. Keep L at a fork. **⑫** Through gate into field-corner and fork L up green track to another gate. Continue up to barn. **⑬** From LH side of barn turn sharp L (60°) to climb thin path on RH side of bank and ditch. On reaching * (bank at

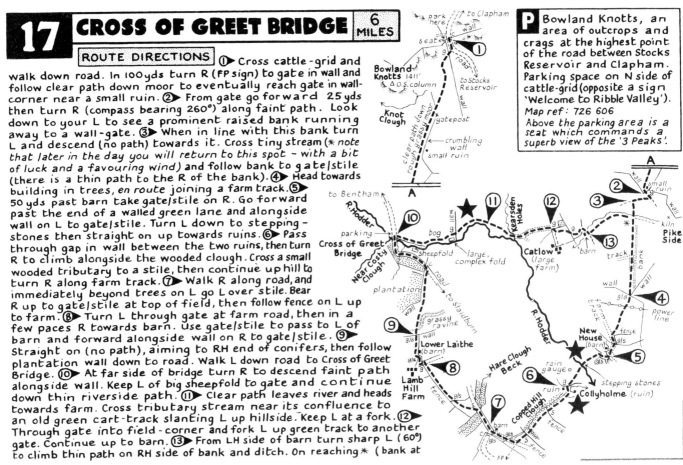

P Bowland Knotts, an area of outcrops and crags at the highest point of the road between Stocks Reservoir and Clapham. Parking space on N side of cattle-grid (opposite a sign 'Welcome to Ribble Valley). Map ref: 726 606
Above the parking area is a seat which commands a superb view of the '3 Peaks'.

Exposed and quite strenuous, with just over 1000' of climbing. Much of the route is pathless and rough underfoot, and there will be boggy sections after rain. No ladder-stiles. ⅓ mile on quiet motor-roads. The path across the moor between points ① and ②, though clear, has hidden ruts beneath the grass – potentially ankle-twisting. This section may be avoided (see 'A SHORTER ALTERNATIVE' below). When the river is high the stepping-stones below New House will be submerged (author's tip – take a couple of plastic bin-liners, just in case). The walk is not recommended in mist.

right-angles on R) turn L (no path) up hillside. On reaching a path turn R along it to return to the gate at point ②. Follow the path used on the outward route up the moor to Bowland Knotts.

A SHORTER ALTERNATIVE

Bowland Knotts is an attractive place to park, with magnificent views, but it does have the disadvantage of being the highest point of the walk. If you don't fancy a lengthy uphill finish you may prefer to do just the circular section of the walk (3¾ miles), in which case park at Cross of Greet Bridge and start at point ⑩. There is parking space on the N side of the bridge, which is 4¼ miles N of Slaidburn on the Bentham road (Map ref: 702 589).

NEW HOUSE AND COLLYHOLME

were once neighbouring hamlets, but the only building which remains intact is the barn illustrated. It bears the date 1814, and the cattle-stalls within could well be original. Between the two bygone settlements the youthful Hodder chuckles merrily along through sequestered pastures, and this is the prettiest place on the walk – a truly peaceful and Arcadian scene.

O.S. MAPS **BD** FOR NOTES ON *THE RIVER HODDER* SEE WALK 23

Cross of Greet

is an ancient monastic cross of which only the base now remains. The stone is over 5' long and has a socket-hole into which the shaft of the cross was fitted. It will not, however, be seen on the walk, for it stands at the summit of the Slaidburn-Bentham road about 1¾ miles NW of the bridge which bears its name. CROSS OF GREET BRIDGE is the first bridge over the Hodder. It is of no great beauty, but is certainly sturdy – as indeed it needs to be to withstand the rigours of ice, storm and flood in this wild and desolate place.

18 LITTLEDALE 6½ MILES

P Little Cragg, a spacious parking area almost at the highest point of the lane between Brookhouse and Quernmore. Map ref: 545 617

For those who prefer to start a walk at its lowest point, there is a small space (3 cars) at Udale Bridge (554 622)

ROUTE DIRECTIONS

① Walk eastwards along the road, which first rises to cross a cattle-grid, then makes a long descent to cross two bridges before rising to a T-junction at New House Farm. ② Turn R (SP Littledale) and walk through the hamlet of Crossgill. ③ Where road bends sharp L fork R to gate/stile (wm) and along green track. On emerging from trees, track goes straight ahead across fields, passing derelict church. ④ At fork keep L (wm) uphill. ⑤ After passing below wood ignore gate into field; keep to RH side of wall/fence. Through small gate (wm) and forward along path between fence and wood. When trees end keep straight on along thin path (wm) in bracken, eventually dropping R to reach footbridge and ladder-stile. ⑥ Don't cross these. Turn around and walk downstream on clear riverside path. ⑦ Turn L over bridge and up farm road to L of buildings. Swing R through farmyard then L (look for arrows). At last barn on R turn R through small gate (wm) and descend clear path. ⑧ Cross footbridge and in a few yards turn R(wm). Look out for steps on L (FP sign) and climb to a stile (wm) at top of wood. Follow edge of field to R. ⑨ Go R over wall-stile (FP sign), pass to R of farm and R (FP sign) to follow farm road to next farm. ⑩ Cross cattle-grid and turn L into farmyard (not house drive). Pass to R of house, take RH of 2 gates and descend with fence on L. At bottom of field turn R. Ford small stream, cross footbridge and forward uphill with wall/fence on R. ⑪ Go R over gate/stile and up an (initially) clear path, rising to climb by LH field boundary. Cross beck and forward to wall-corner. ⑫ (For SHORT FINISH see above left). Turn L and climb clear path to ladder-stile and access notice. ⑬ Turn R and head for prominent green path slanting up hillside. On nearing top branch R

SHORT FINISH

⑫ At the wall-corner go straight ahead. Pass through gate to R of barnyard and bear R on slightly raised path. Go through gate/stile (wm) and follow wall on L to another gate/stile. Follow cart-track up LH side of wall. Through gate/stile (wm) by small barn and up to ladder-stile.

Former chapel of St.Ann (1751) now converted into a private residence (Old Church House) of novel appearance.

After crossing a slab bridge you could turn down R to join the lower (return) path. Use this short cut in wet weather to avoid boggy ground further upstream.

(map labels) Caton · New House Farm ② · Artle Beck · Fostal Bridge · Crossgill · Udale Bridge · Foxdale Beck · Udale Beck · small barn · ③ · derelict church · ④ ⑤ · broken wall · ⑥ · wall · gls · Littledale Hall · ⑦ · farm road · boggy · FB and ladder-stile · Little Cragg Parking Area · Baines Cragg · Bark Barn · FP · Cragg Farm · small barn · wall · ① · ⑩ · farm road · ⑧ · ⑨ · R.Conder · FB · ⑮ · Cragg Wood · (not a tidy farm) · Bellhill · Skelbow Barn · ⑫ · Udale Beck · official right-of-way (but the farmer would probably prefer you to use the road) · Field Head (a tidy farm) · prominent outcrop · ⑭ · heather · grouse butt · shooters track · ⑬ · ⑪ · ACCESS AREA · R.Conder · wall-corner. ⑫

18

👢 Undulating walk and fairly strenuous, especially if long finish via Access Area (NO DOGS) is included. Rich variety of terrain and mostly clear paths and tracks. Parts of the section between points ⑤ and ⑦ may be overgrown with rampant bracken in high summer and boggy in wet weather. The full route has 1¾ miles of motor-road walking (very little traffic) and 5 ladder-stiles (2 with adjacent gates). The two short-cuts shown on the map will reduce the walk to 4¼ miles (1⅓ miles of road-walking and 1 ladder-stile with adjacent gate).

along thin path through heather. Keep about 30yds from the edge on the R, then turn L up a clearer path and head towards a prominent rock edge. Pass well to the L of it. ⑭▶ Turn R down a wide vehicle track. ⑮▶ Branch R off track just before reaching house and cross slab bridge to ladder-stile. Climb through gorse to another ladder-stile and walk R up road back to car park.

LITTLEDALE IS UNQUESTIONABLY ONE OF THE LOVELIEST LOCALITIES IN THE WHOLE OF BOWLAND – A PLACE OF EXQUISITE CHARM WHATEVER THE SEASON. HERE ARE TINY, PEACEFUL AND SEEMINGLY FORGOTTEN VALLEYS SET AGAINST A COLOURFUL BACKCLOTH OF WILD AND RUGGED FELLS. SPARKLING STREAMS, HAVING TUMBLED AND SPLASHED DOWN THE STEEP SLOPES OF WARD'S STONE AND CLOUGHA, NOW FLOW MORE SEDATELY THROUGH SYLVAN WOODLANDS ON THEIR WAY NORTHWARDS TO JOIN THE LUNE

LITTLEDALE HALL and its various satellite buildings are typically Victorian, and were built c 1840-50 by John Dodson, Vicar of Cockerham and son of a Liverpudlian shipping magnate.

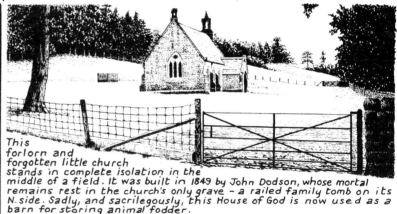

This forlorn and forgotten little church stands in complete isolation in the middle of a field. It was built in 1849 by John Dodson, whose mortal remains rest in the church's only grave – a railed family tomb on its N. side. Sadly, and sacrilegously, this House of God is now used as a barn for storing animal fodder.

UDALE BECK and FOXDALE BECK unite at Udale Bridge to form ARTLE BECK, which flows for 3½ miles to enter the Lune at Caton.

ACCESS AREA · · · **RESTRICTIONS**

O.S.MAP **A**

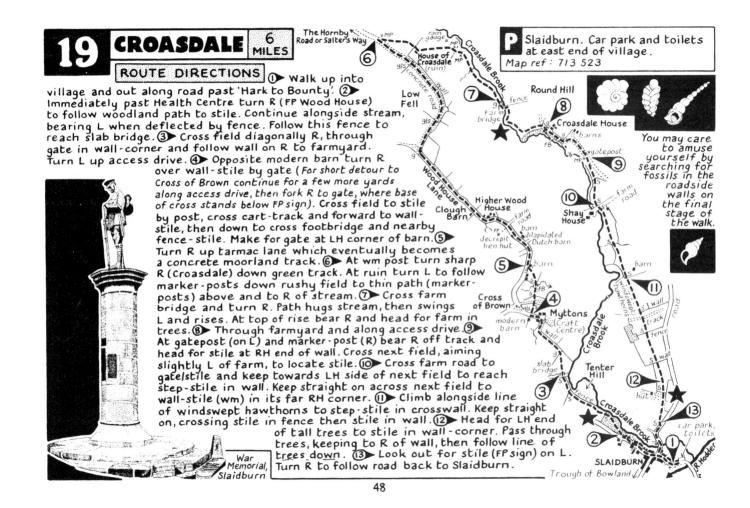

19 CROASDALE — 6 MILES

The Hornby Road or Salter's Way

P Slaidburn. Car park and toilets at east end of village. Map ref: 713 523

ROUTE DIRECTIONS

① Walk up into village and out along road past 'Hark to Bounty'. ② Immediately past Health Centre turn R (FP Wood House) to follow woodland path to stile. Continue alongside stream, bearing L when deflected by fence. Follow this fence to reach slab bridge. ③ Cross field diagonally R, through gate in wall-corner and follow wall on R to farmyard. Turn L up access drive. ④ Opposite modern barn turn R over wall-stile by gate (*For short detour to Cross of Brown continue for a few more yards along access drive, then fork R to gate, where base of cross stands below FP sign*). Cross field to stile by post, cross cart-track and forward to wall-stile, then down to cross footbridge and nearby fence-stile. Make for gate at LH corner of barn. ⑤ Turn R up tarmac lane which eventually becomes a concrete moorland track. ⑥ At wm post turn sharp R (Croasdale) down green track. At ruin turn L to follow marker-posts down rushy field to thin path (marker-posts) above and to R of stream. ⑦ Cross farm bridge and turn R. Path hugs stream, then swings L and rises. At top of rise bear R and head for farm in trees. ⑧ Through farmyard and along access drive. ⑨ At gatepost (on L) and marker-post (R) bear R off track and head for stile at RH end of wall. Cross next field, aiming slightly L of farm, to locate stile. ⑩ Cross farm road to gate/stile and keep towards LH side of next field to reach step-stile in wall. Keep straight on across next field to wall-stile (wm) in its far RH corner. ⑪ Climb alongside line of windswept hawthorns to step-stile in crosswall. Keep straight on, crossing stile in fence then stile in wall. ⑫ Head for LH end of tall trees to stile in wall-corner. Pass through trees, keeping to R of wall, then follow line of trees down. ⑬ Look out for stile (FP sign) on L. Turn R to follow road back to Slaidburn.

You may care to amuse yourself by searching for fossils in the roadside walls on the final stage of the walk.

War Memorial, Slaidburn

SLAIDBURN
Trough of Bowland

19

Easy walking with very gentle gradients. Contrasting terrain of lush pasture and bleak moorland. Some potentially boggy places, particularly in upper reaches of Croasdale. ½ mile on motor-roads, ¾ mile on traffic-free tarmac lane, ¾ mile on concrete/tarmac moorland track. 2 ladder-stiles, both with adjacent gates.

SLAIDBURN

may justifiably claim recognition as 'The Capital of Bowland'. Reposing twixt the banks of the Hodder and Croasdale Brook, this ancient sheep-farming settlement is hugely popular with visitors, who find enchantment in wandering among the 16/17th C. cottages and cobbled forecourts. In bygone days the village had its own smithy and wheelwright, and over the years Slaidburn has seen an assortment of industries flourish and decline. Hats, shoes and dresses have been made here, and once there was a tannery and a corn mill. The lovely old pub supposedly owes its curious name to an imbibing 19th C. squire who, on recognizing the sound of baying in the distance as that of his favourite hound, exclaimed 'Hark to Bounty!' Called 'The Dog Inn' prior to 1875, it was once the home of the Forest Courts, and the old courtroom has been preserved. It is reached by the door above the outside steps, and contains oak benches, dock, witness box and open timberwork ceiling.

Hark to Bounty

FOR NOTES ON SLAIDBURN CHURCH SEE WALK 10

CROASDALE

WILL APPEAL TO ALL THOSE WITH A PREDILECTION FOR BLEAK AND LONELY PLACES. THE SOMBRE VALLEY HAS A WILD, SEVERE BEAUTY WHICH IN LATE SUMMER, WHEN THE MOOR IS A SEA OF PURPLE, BECOMES AN EXTRAVAGANT BEAUTY WHICH WILL UPLIFT THE SOUL. THE LIVELY CROASDALE BROOK IS ONE OF THE HODDER'S MAJOR TRIBUTARIES.

Croasdale Bridge

Cross of Brown

is of monastic origin, but don't expect anything eye-catching or you'll be sadly disappointed. All that remains is the base with its shaft-socket — moss-covered, lichen-encrusted and in danger of becoming completely overgrown.

FOR NOTES ON THE HORNBY ROAD SEE WALK 29

HOUSE OF CROASDALE was built in the mid-17th C — possibly on the site of a medieval hunting-lodge — and was formerly called Hill House. Totally exposed to the elements, its moldering, windswept ruins can assume, in certain weather conditions, a 'Wuthering Heights' type of menacing atmosphere. The author can personally vouch for this, having once been caught there in a sudden, violent electrical storm. Not a pleasant experience.

THE MOOR is a nesting-ground and habitat for many species of bird.

PLEASE ● keep to the paths.

● keep your dog under close control.

● walk as quietly as possible, especially during the breeding-season (April-June).

Lapwing

O.S. MAP D

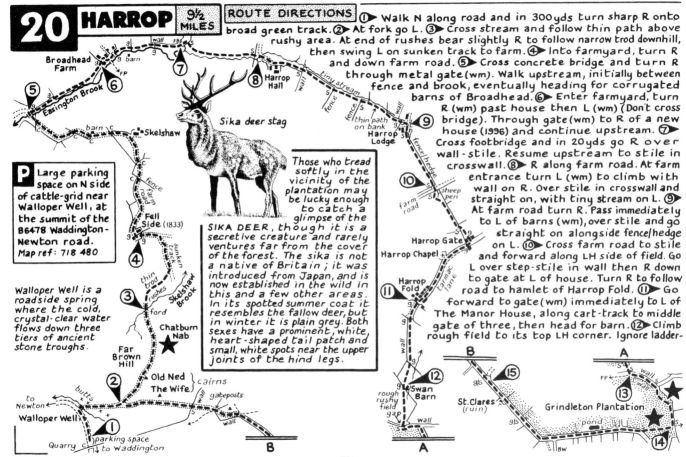

20 HARROP 9½ MILES

① Walk N along road and in 300yds turn sharp R onto broad green track. ② At fork go L. ③ Cross stream and follow thin path above rushy area. At end of rushes bear slightly R to follow narrow trod downhill, then swing L on sunken track to farm. ④ Into farmyard, turn R and down farm road. ⑤ Cross concrete bridge and turn R through metal gate(wm). Walk upstream, initially between fence and brook, eventually heading for corrugated barns of Broadhead. ⑥ Enter farmyard, turn R (wm) past house then L (wm) (Don't cross bridge). Through gate(wm) to R of a new house (1996) and continue upstream. ⑦ Cross footbridge and in 20yds go R over wall-stile. Resume upstream to stile in crosswall. ⑧ R along farm road. At farm entrance turn L (wm) to climb with wall on R. Over stile in crosswall and straight on, with tiny stream on L. ⑨ At farm road turn R. Pass immediately to L of barns (wm), over stile and go straight on alongside fence/hedge on L. ⑩ Cross farm road to stile and forward along LH side of field. Go L over step-stile in wall then R down to gate at L of house. Turn R to follow road to hamlet of Harrop Fold. ⑪ Go forward to gate(wm) immediately to L of The Manor House, along cart-track to middle gate of three, then head for barn. ⑫ Climb rough field to its top LH corner. Ignore ladder-

Broadhead Farm

FP

barn

wall FB

Easington Brook

Skelshaw

Sika deer stag

barn

fence

farm road

Fall Side (1833)

thin trod

rushes

sunken track

Skelshaw Brook

ford

Harrop Hall

tiny stream

fence

wall

thin path on bank

Harrop Lodge

fence/hedge

farm road

sheep pen

Harrop Gate

Harrop Chapel

Harrop Fold

tarmac lane

wall

P Large parking space on N side of cattle-grid near Walloper Well, at the summit of the B6478 Waddington-Newton road. Map ref: 718 480

Walloper Well is a roadside spring where the cold, crystal-clear water flows down three tiers of ancient stone troughs.

Those who tread softly in the vicinity of the plantation may be lucky enough to catch a glimpse of the SIKA DEER, though it is a secretive creature and rarely ventures far from the cover of the forest. The sika is not a native of Britain; it was introduced from Japan, and is now established in the wild in this and a few other areas. In its spotted summer coat it resembles the fallow deer, but in winter it is plain grey. Both sexes have a prominent, white, heart-shaped tail patch and small, white spots near the upper joints of the hind legs.

Far Brown Hill

Chatburn Nab

Old Ned The Wife

cairns

gateposts

wall

to Newton

butts

Walloper Well

parking space

Quarry

to Waddington

B

rough rushy field gap

Swan Barn

wall

A

B

St. Clares (ruin)

⑮

Grindleton Plantation

FP

wall

⑬

pond

BW

⑭

A

50

20

No steep gradients, but a long and quite tiring walk, with most of the 700' of uphill work occuring on the final section from Swan Barn onwards. Very varied terrain, including pathless pastures, farm roads, lanes, forest paths and some splendid moorland tracks. 1 small ladder-stile. Motor-road walking negligible.

stile. Go up through gap in crosswall, over fence-stile and turn L (wm). Walk between wall and trees, then turn R (wm) alongside broken wall. ⑬ Turn L along grassy track between walls. At wooden stile turn R to follow path along edge of plantation. ⑭ At stile in wall on L turn R into trees to follow waymarked path to stile. Turn R along road. ⑮ When road turns R go straight on through gate/stile and up rough track. Ignore walled track going L. At wall-corner fork L. At gateposts follow RH track over iron ladder-stile in crosswall and across moor to point ②.

HARROP

REFERENCES TO HARROP ('VALLEY OF HARES') GO BACK TO THE 13TH CENTURY. IN THOSE FAR-OFF DAYS IT WAS ONE OF THE FOUR 'WARDS OF THE ROYAL FOREST OF BOWLAND (THE OTHERS WERE BASHALL, SLAIDBURN AND CHIPPING). THE LONELY FARMSTEAD OF **HARROP HALL** WAS BUILT DURING THE 17TH AND EARLY 18TH CENTURIES. BOTH THE MAIN DOORWAY AND THAT OF ONE OF THE BARNS CARRY THE DATE 1719. THE DELIGHTFUL **HARROP CHAPEL**, BUILT 1820-1 (ILLUSTRATED ABOVE), HAS THE DISTINCTION OF BEING THE OLDEST METHODIST CHAPEL IN THE AREA STILL IN USE. ABOUT 1850 A MR. THOMAS LORD MOVED INTO ITS ADJOINING COTTAGE AND THERE ESTABLISHED A DAY SCHOOL WHICH OPERATED UNTIL 1874 AND BECAME KNOWN LOCALLY AS 'LORD'S ACADEMY'. A SHORT STROLL ALONG THE TARMAC LANE BRINGS US TO THE SECLUDED LITTLE HAMLET OF **HARROP FOLD**, WHERE OUR ROUTE PASSES BETWEEN TWO OF ITS OLDEST BUILDINGS. THE LARGE WHITE HOUSE ON THE LEFT WAS AN ORIGINAL LANCASHIRE LONGHOUSE BUILT IN THE 17TH CENTURY, AND THE MANOR HOUSE, OPPOSITE, IS OF THE SAME VINTAGE.

Easington Brook

Skelshaw

Not many cairns can boast personal names, and you would therefore expect **OLD NED** and **THE WIFE** to be quite impressive structures. You'll be sorely disappointed. They're feeble efforts to say the least, but they possibly mark ancient burial mounds.

O.S. MAPS D F **ST. CLARES**, ONCE A REMOTE FARMSTEAD (WITH A FINE VIEW), IS NOW BUT A FEW HEAPS OF RUBBLE.

21 ROEBURNDALE 5½ MILES

P Barkin Bridge, most easily reached by a lane (SP Roeburndale West) which leaves the B6480 1 mile W of Wray. There are small roadside parking spaces on either side of the bridge.
Map ref: 600 637

ROUTE DIRECTIONS

① Walk along the road up-valley. ② Turn L (FP sign) at chapel. Straight through farmyard to gate and cart-track. At its end go forward up RH side of fence (wm) to gate in crosswall and green track between fences. ③ Cross field to stile about 60 yds to R of power-line, then straight on across next field. ④ At a big depression turn sharp R (more than 90°) and climb to stile in crosswall. Forward with wall on L to stile in crossfence, then cross next field diagonally R. Over two neighbouring ladder-stiles at field corner then head for farm. ⑤ Go L up lane for a few yards, then turn R to pass between wall and barns to a gate. Descend field to gate in front of barn, then turn L to follow farm road into farmyard (Mallowdale). ⑥ Pass between house and barn. At end of buildings go R through gates, then turn L and descend field to locate stile and footbridge over Mallow Gill. ⑦ Turn R to climb thin path to stile above trees. Turn R to follow fence, cross wall-stile (with benchmark) then turn L up small field to gate. ⑧ Keep L to gate just in front of farmhouse, turn R out of farm, then straight across field (no path), under power-line, to gate/stile in crossfence. In next field keep close to LH fence to reach stile in corner by tiny stream. ⑨ Go straight on up a slight depression (to R of a group of 3 trees). Maintain height, passing to R of a pair of trees, to locate stile in crosswall. In next field maintain direction uphill, and when a barn comes into view head towards it. ⑩ Before end of field you will reach an old, green cart-track. Turn very sharp R to double back along top of field (wm) to stile in wall corner. Forward with wall on L. ⑪ At modern barn go through small gate (above steps), turn R then R again along tarmac road. ⑫ Fork L along farm road. Don't enter farmyard. Follow cart-track on L of fence. ⑬ Beyond a small plantation cross to other side of broken wall and go to gate at fence-corner. Bear R (compass 30°) and aim for 2nd uppermost tree visible in ravine ahead. Cross stream just to L of it. ⑭ Climb steep bank

When descending from Thornbush the wooded valley seen beyond the barn is Pedder Gill.

Hill Barn is dropping to bits and dangerous — keep away.

You could turn R here to follow the wall up, and thus avoid climbing 2 wall-stiles (the second of which is b_____ awkward) but it's not the true right-of-way.

⑯ Thornbush
pine trees
barn
⑮
wall
lone tree
⑭ Warm Beck
fence
⑬
young plantation
Crosley Gill Beck
R. Roeburn
Barkin Bridge
Meth. Chapel
Hill Barn
probably mucky
barn
Winder
barn (1672)
Roeburndale Road
⑫
barn
gle
Swaintley Hill
⑪
⑩
wall
⑨
fence
boggy
fence
short cut to point 12
short cut to point 1
⑧
gls
Haylot Farm
⑦
⑥
Mallowdale
Mallow Gill
Saltar Clough Beck
Mallowdale Bridge
R. Roeburn
barn
High Salter
barns
⑤
old car
wall
fence
④ big, rushy depression
③
②
①
Lower Salter
to Haylot Farm
road
wall

21

An undulating walk mostly on farm roads and pathless pastures, with beautiful views. Route-finding needs care in places. 2 ladder-stiles and 2 or 3 awkward wall-stiles. ¾ of a mile on motor-roads (virtually traffic-free). The second half of the walk (Haylot onwards) is not recommended in mist. Two SHORT CUTS are available from Haylot : a) Down the farm road to point ① (reducing the walk to 3¼ miles) or b) Up the farm road to point ⑫ (5 miles).

to stile in crosswall. Straight on (compass 42°) over hill and make for gate at fence-corner. ⑮► Don't use gate, but walk along top side of fence to join an old green cart-track. Follow it down alongside pine trees then L to the farm. ⑯► At farmyard entrance (by 2 old railway wagons) take metal gate on R and descend diagonally R to gate near barn. Go R along road to Barkin Bridge.

ROEBURNDALE

Convolvulus or Bindweed – grows in profusion around Barkin Bridge.

This is a typical Bowland valley; peaceful, unspoilt and exquisitely beautiful. Much of upper Roeburndale is open moorland, but the courses of the river and its tributaries are attractively wooded. Try to visit these woodlands when they are carpeted with spring flowers or even better – when they are aflame with the glorious reds, yellows, russets and golds of autumn. Keeping vigil over the head of the valley is the shapely Mallowdale Pike. Its graceful outline bids the walker 'Come hither', but sadly, like so many Bowland hills, it carries no rights-of-way. The River Roeburn rises on the wild heights of Mallowdale Fell and flows for some eight miles to join the Hindburn at Wray. Though normally just a gentle, babbling brook *it has potentially devastating power,* as was seen on 8th. August 1967. On that fateful day the Roeburn became a raging torrent; flood water swept down the valley, destroying bridges and farm buildings and washing away cottages in Wray.

● The barn in the RH field-corner at Haylot Farm has a doorhead with the date 1669 and a small star.

● ON YOUR DRIVE UP-VALLEY TO BARKIN BRIDGE LOOK OUT FOR A TINY ROADSIDE CROSS. IT'S ON THE LH VERGE ABOUT ½ MILE FROM THE B6480 JUNCTION.

The tiny chapel at Lower Salter

O. S. MAPS A B

WINDER, a sombre farmstead. Note in passing the 1669 doorhead and the old grindstone.

A doorhead dated 1658 reveals the antiquity of the lonely hillside farm of **HIGH SALTER**. Here the lane loses its tarmac surface and continues towards the high fells as a rough-metalled track. This is the northern end of the **SALTER'S WAY**, an ancient packhorse route once used by salt carriers en route from Morecambe Bay to the inland farms and villages of Bowland and the Ribble Valley. In crossing the fells to Slaidburn the track provides one of the finest moorland walks in the country. The southern end of the Salter's Way features in Walk 29.

Approaching High Salter

P Bolton-by-Bowland. Car park and toilets at W end of village. Map ref: 784 493

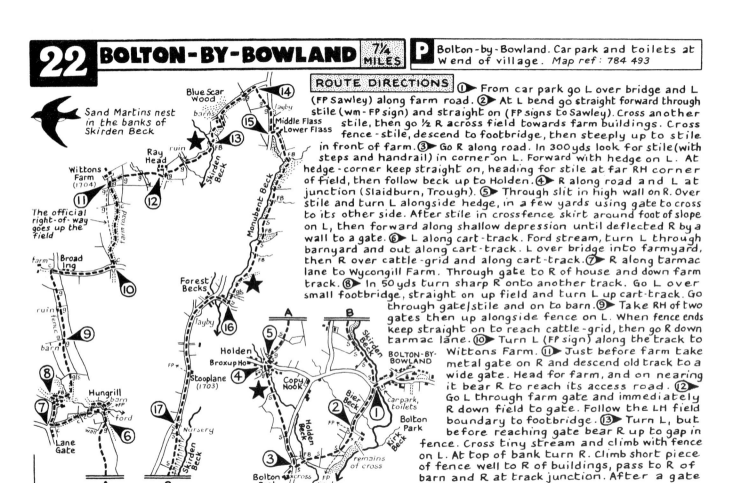

Blue Scar Wood

barns

Sand Martins nest in the banks of Skirden Beck

Middle Flass
Lower Flass

Ray Head

ruin

Wittons Farm (1704)

Skirden Beck

Monubent Beck

The official right-of-way goes up the field

Broad Ing

farm

ruin

barn

Forest Becks

layby

Holden
Broxup Ho

Stooplane (1703)

Hungrill
barn
ford
wall

Lane Gate

Nursery

Skirden Beck

A   B

Bolton Peel

cross

FP Sawley

remains of cross

Copy Nook

Bier Beck

Holden Beck

Kirk Beck

Bolton Park

carpark, toilets

BOLTON-BY-BOWLAND

Skirden Beck

ROUTE DIRECTIONS

① From car park go L over bridge and L (FP Sawley) along farm road. ② At L bend go straight forward through stile (wm - FP sign) and straight on (FP signs to Sawley). Cross another stile, then go ½ R across field towards farm buildings. Cross fence - stile, descend to footbridge, then steeply up to stile in front of farm. ③ Go R along road. In 300 yds look for stile (with steps and handrail) in corner on L. Forward with hedge on L. At hedge - corner keep straight on, heading for stile at far RH corner of field, then follow beck up to Holden. ④ R along road and L at junction (Slaidburn, Trough). ⑤ Through slit in high wall on R. Over stile and turn L alongside hedge, in a few yards using gate to cross to its other side. After stile in crossfence skirt around foot of slope on L, then forward along shallow depression until deflected R by a wall to a gate. ⑥ L along cart-track. Ford stream, turn L through barnyard and out along cart-track. L over bridge into farmyard, then R over cattle-grid and along cart-track. ⑦ R along tarmac lane to Wycongill Farm. Through gate to R of house and down farm track. ⑧ In 50 yds turn sharp R onto another track. Go L over small footbridge, straight on up field and turn L up cart-track. Go through gate/stile and on to barn. ⑨ Take RH of two gates then up alongside fence on L. When fence ends keep straight on to reach cattle-grid, then go R down tarmac lane. ⑩ Turn L (FP sign) along the track to Wittons Farm. ⑪ Just before farm take metal gate on R and descend old track to a wide gate. Head for farm, and on nearing it bear R to reach its access road. ⑫ Go L through farm gate and immediately R down field to gate. Follow the LH field boundary to footbridge. ⑬ Turn L, but before reaching gate bear R up to gap in fence. Cross tiny stream and climb with fence on L. At top of bank turn R. Climb short piece of fence well to R of buildings, pass to R of barn and R at track junction. After a gate

Easy walking, mainly through pastures, with some attractive riverside sections. Route-finding a bit complicated in places. No ladder-stiles. 1¼ miles on motor-roads.

the track becomes enclosed by hedges. ⑭ Turn R through wide gap in hedge and cross field to its far LH corner. Turn R along road. ⑮ Turn L (FP sign) and fork R through gate on R of small barn. Straight on along field then drop to footbridge. Turn R to follow permissive path (white arrows) alongside beck. ⑯ Turn R along cart-track then L along road. ⑰ At nurseries go L over stile (FP sign) and follow fence down to another stile. Go straight on across next field, keeping to high ground. Follow the beck, passing through a series of fence-stiles (some not easy to find), down to stile at Skirden Bridge, opposite car-park.

BOLTON-BY-BOWLAND

This is one of the region's prettiest and most historic villages. Listed in the Domesday Book, it was granted a market charter by Edward III in 1354, and a market was held here until the turn of the present century. The PARISH CHURCH is an absolute gem and must not be missed. It dates back at least to the 13th C, but was extensively rebuilt c 1464 by Sir Ralph Pudsay, whose tomb is quite remarkable. Fashioned in black limestone, it depicts Sir Ralph, his three (consecutive!) wives and his twenty-five children. Each wife has, in the folds of her dress, a numeral indicating the number of children she bore to Sir Ralph - Matilda 2, Margaret 6 and Edwina 17. Several pews bear the date 1694 and the initials of their first owners. The studded oak door is dated 1705 and the font is early 16th C. KEYS COTTAGE, one of the many quaint cottages set haphazardly along the main street, is dated 1716 and is so named because of the unusual design on its doorhead. The VILLAGE GREEN boasts a medieval cross, stocks and two large millstones. At the E. end of the village is a second green · SCHOOL GREEN - which was once used for the annual fair. The COACH AND HORSES is a most convivial early 13th C. inn. The OLD RECTORY is thought to date from the late 17th C.

O.S. MAP D F

BOLTON PEEL

is a sturdy, 17th century farmhouse by which stands a fine preaching cross set in an ancient base. From the Peel family of Bolton Peel came Sir Robert (Prime Minister 1834-5, 1841-6). As Home Secretary he founded the modern police force (the term 'bobby' is derived from his name).

Stooplane (Stoop Lane on O.S. maps)

The waterfall just below the pretty hamlet of HOLDEN can look quite impressive when in spate. Make a short detour L at point ④ to view the splendid Broxup House (1687).

THE NEIGHBOURING FARMS OF HUNGRILL AND WYCONGILL BOTH DATE FROM THE 17th C.

SKIRDEN BECK is liable to sudden changes in level, and has flooded on many occasions.

The path alongside **MONUBENT BECK** is a permissive one made available through the Countryside Stewardship Scheme, which offers financial assistance to landowners who are prepared to help in conserving our countryside, its wildlife and historic features. At Monubent Beck the aim is to encourage a variety of flowers and grasses to recolonise the area.

23 BEATRIX 5 MILES

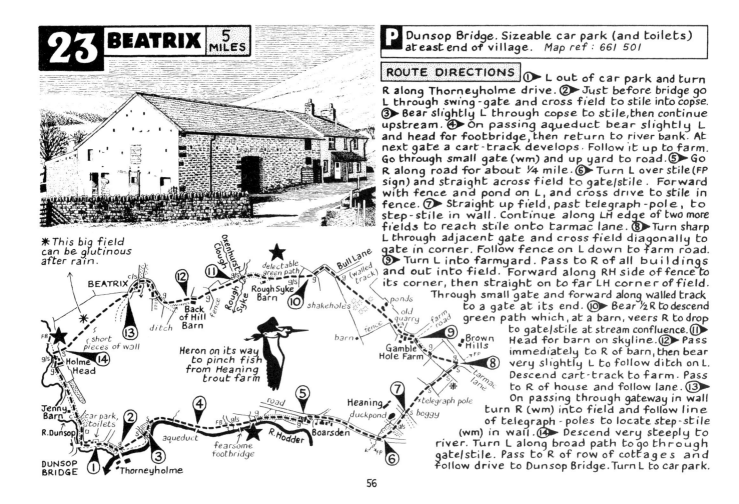

P Dunsop Bridge. Sizeable car park (and toilets) at east end of village. Map ref: 661 501

ROUTE DIRECTIONS

① L out of car park and turn R along Thorneyholme drive. ② Just before bridge go L through swing-gate and cross field to stile into copse. ③ Bear slightly L through copse to stile, then continue upstream. ④ On passing aqueduct bear slightly L and head for footbridge, then return to river bank. At next gate a cart-track develops. Follow it up to farm. Go through small gate (wm) and up yard to road. ⑤ Go R along road for about ¼ mile. ⑥ Turn L over stile (FP sign) and straight across field to gate/stile. Forward with fence and pond on L, and cross drive to stile in fence. ⑦ Straight up field, past telegraph-pole, to step-stile in wall. Continue along LH edge of two more fields to reach stile onto tarmac lane. ⑧ Turn sharp L through adjacent gate and cross field diagonally to gate in corner. Follow fence on L down to farm road. ⑨ Turn L into farmyard. Pass to R of all buildings and out into field. Forward along RH side of fence to its corner, then straight on to far LH corner of field. Through small gate and forward along walled track to a gate at its end. ⑩ Bear ½ R to descend green path which, at a barn, veers R to drop to gate/stile at stream confluence. ⑪ Head for barn on skyline. ⑫ Pass immediately to R of barn, then bear very slightly L to follow ditch on L. Descend cart-track to farm. Pass to R of house and follow lane. ⑬ On passing through gateway in wall turn R (wm) into field and follow line of telegraph-poles to locate step-stile (wm) in wall. ⑭ Descend very steeply to river. Turn L along broad path to go through gate/stile. Pass to R of row of cottages and follow drive to Dunsop Bridge. Turn L to car park.

*This big field can be glutinous after rain.

Heron on its way to pinch fish from Heaning trout farm

BEATRIX

ovenhurst Clough

Bull Lane (walled track)

Rough Syke Barn

Back of Hill Barn

ditch

Rough Syke

shakeholes

ponds

old quarry

barn   fence

farm road

Brown Hills

Gamble Hole Farm

short pieces of wall

Holme Head

Jenny Barn

R. Dunsop

car park, toilets

aqueduct

fearsome footbridge

road

R. Hodder

Boarsden

Heaning

duckpond

boggy

telegraph pole

tarmac lane

DUNSOP BRIDGE

Thorneyholme

Riverside meadows and undulating hillside pastures – mostly pathless. Easy walking, with no steep gradients (apart from the short descent at point ⑭). No ladder-stiles. ¼ mile on a motor-road between points ⑤ and ⑥ – take care, especially if walking a dog.

23

THORNEYHOLME HALL, now a health farm and once a nunnery, is a Victorian mansion originally owned by the Towneleys, a family which made a fortune from racehorses. Their most famous horse was KETTLEDRUM, winner of the Derby in 1861.

Thorneyholme Hall
HEALTH SPA
TEL. 0200 - 448271

Prominent up on your left during the early stages of the walk is a curiously-shaped limestone outcrop named on the O.S. map as 'KNOT or SUGAR LOAF.' In days of yore a gibbet stood on Sugar Loaf, exhibiting from time to time the rotting corpses of local miscreants who had received a suspended sentence. Keep a sharp lookout for the boggart which is said to haunt the area.

THE HODDER is Lancashire's loveliest river – sparkling and unpolluted throughout its rural course. A major tributary of the Ribble, it is born on the slopes of Lamb Hill Fell, just above Cross of Greet Bridge on the Slaidburn - Bentham road. After passing through the huge Stocks Reservoir, the Hodder glides serenely through flowery meadows below Slaidburn, Newton and the picturesque little village of Dunsop Bridge. At Whitewell the hitherto gentle river rushes headlong through a wooded limestone gorge, then flows sedately once more through pastures and woodlands to join the Ribble just below Great Mitton.

GAMBLE HOLE FARM'S peculiar name has given rise to some fanciful speculation, but is most probably derived from GAMEL, a Norse personal name. The farm has a datestone inscribed WW 1845. The huge, deep hole in the field just above the farm is the remains of an underground chamber whose roof has collapsed. The depression has been quarried for limestone.

This unusual stile (marked # on the map) is a helluva tight squeeze.

BEATRIX HAS BEEN A STOCK-REARING CENTRE SINCE THE EARLY 13TH C., AND WAS ONCE A BUSY HAMLET – MARKETS WERE HELD HERE IN THE SEVENTEENTH AND EIGHTEENTH CENTURIES. SEVERAL 17TH C. DOORHEADS AND WINDOW MULLIONS ARE BUILT INTO THE SURROUNDING FARM WALLS, AND THERE ARE FAINT TRACES OF THE GRASSED-OVER FOUNDATIONS OF LONG-VANISHED DWELLINGS.

O.S. MAP **D**

FOR NOTES ON DUNSOP BRIDGE SEE WALK 4.

24 STONYHURST & LONGRIDGE FELL 8¼ MILES

ROUTE DIRECTIONS

P Kemple End. Roadside parking space just above hamlet near top of Birdy Brow. Map ref: 688 405

① Walk down road and at L bend go forward onto gravel track. Swing R past Kemple Cottage then L down farm lane. ② In field follow LH hedge to stile at fence-corner, then RH hedge to another stile. Drop to house and L along access drive. Turn R along road. ③ To visit College detour L through lodge gates (FP sign) and down drive. Return to continue along road and turn L down Hurst Green road. ④ Turn R (FP sign) through car park and onto golf course. Follow brick-edged path, and when bricks end fork L. Pass around LH side of walled wood then bear L to drop to gate/stile in wood corner. ⑤ Cross foot-bridge to path curving R up bank to gate/stile. Climb to farm, turn L through gate, then take LH of two gates and cross field to stile into wood. ⑥ Descend to footbridge and up very steep bank to ladder-stile. Forward to reach farm road via two stiles. Turn R, and at Greengore continue straight ahead alongside plantation. Ignore gate into wood. ⑦ After passing alongside high wire fence on L, go through gate/stile and turn L up rough pasture to ladder-stile on skyline between two plantations. Turn ½ R to cross field diagonally to stile in fence corner, then up to top LH corner of next field. ⑧ Go L along road, then turn R (FP sign)

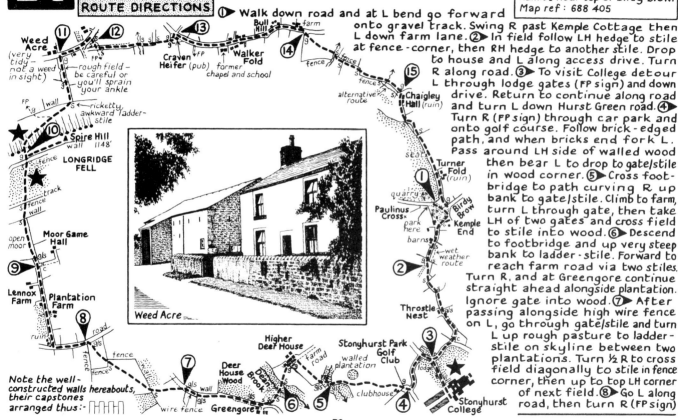

Weed Acre (very tidy – not a weed in sight)

Craven Heifer (pub)

Walker Fold

former chapel and school

Bull Hill

farm

rough field – be careful or you'll sprain your ankle

ricketty, awkward ladder-stile

Spire Hill 1148'

LONGRIDGE FELL

Moor Game Hall

open moor

Lennox Farm

Plantation Farm

ruin

road

Note the well-constructed walls hereabouts, their capstones arranged thus :-

wire fence

Deer House Wood

Greengore

Higher Deer House

Stonyhurst Park Golf Club

walled plantation

clubhouse

Stonyhurst College

Throstle Nest

Paulinus Cross

park here

barns

wet weather route

Kemple End

Birdy Brow

Turner Fold (ruin)

quarry

seat

alternative route

Chaigley Hall (ruin)

fence

Weed Acre

24

Varied terrain, including pastures, a golf course, wooded dells and heather moorland. Fairly strenuous, with one very steep climb at Dean Brook. 1½ miles on quiet motor-roads. 5 ladder-stiles and many small wooden stiles – most of them flimsy and wobbly. Magnificent views across Ribble Valley and Vale of Chipping. Best done late-August, when College is open to the public and heather is in bloom. Allow plenty of time, especially if taking guided tour of College.

up access drive to Moor Game Hall etc. ⑨► When drive turns R to last farm keep straight on along green path to gate/stile onto open moor. Thin, clear path climbs through heather, eventually passing through young plantation to reach gate in ridge-wall. ⑩► A much-used (though not a right-of-way) path goes R along N side of wall to O.S. column at summit. Our path goes forward then slants R down fellside. Cross wall at a ladder-stile and descend to gate into rough, narrow field. Forward to road. ⑪► Walk R along road. ⑫► Pass end of drive to Rakefoot Farm, and about 100yds further on take stile on R in hedge (FP sign). Climb to top of field and turn L along enclosed track. Straight on over several stiles to reach small gate into garden of pub. L through fence-gate to road. ⑬► Walk R along road for a good ½ mile. ⑭► 70yds past farm on L turn R through gate (FP sign) and head towards LH end of fell. Cross tiny ravine and hidden stile, then go forward with fence on L. Cross two stiles and continue with fence now on your R. ⑮► Turn R to pass to R of ruin then follow fence on L. Cross stile and follow path just below plantation to road at Kemple End.

STONYHURST

originally belonged to the Bayley family and later to the Shireburns. The heraldic devices represent these families, for the Bayley arms displayed an eagle and those of the Shireburns a lion. In 1592 Sir Richard Shireburn began to build a new house here which was to remain the family home until the death of the last Shireburn - Sir Nicholas - in 1717. The house fell into disrepair, and in 1794 was handed over to the Society of Jesuits, since when it has been extended and developed to become one of the country's most eminent public schools. The college museum houses some priceless relics of Renaissance times, and the library has some very rare books, including the oldest existing English bound book - a 7th C. copy of St. John's Gospel. The magnificent W. front is flanked by the beautiful St. Peter's Church, built 1832-5 and modelled upon King's College Chapel, Cambridge. Famous ex-pupils include poet Gerard Manley Hopkins, writer Sir Arthur Conan Doyle and actor Charles Laughton.

QUANT IE PLIS

GREENGORE is a fine 17thC house which is reputed to occupy the site of a shooting-lodge belonging to King John (1357-1433). Note the massive buttresses.

CHAIGLEY HALL, with its large barn, was built c1820, but the sad ruins are probably those of a later Victorian house.

LONGRIDGE FELL stands alone and aloof at the southern fringe of Bowland, and is, in fact, Britain's most southerly 'fell'. Dark green conifers and purple heather clothe the slopes of this proud little hill which, because of its isolated position, provides superb panoramic views.

Spire Hill, the summit of Longridge Fell.

O.S. MAPS F G

25 WHELP STONE CRAG 5½ MILES

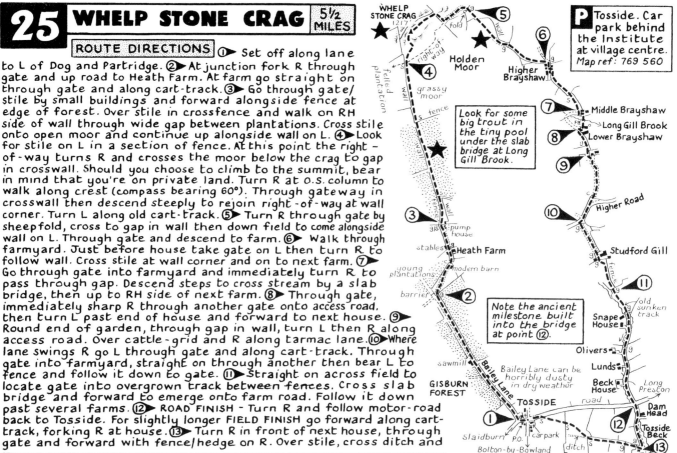

P Tosside. Car park behind the Institute at village centre. Map ref: 769 560

ROUTE DIRECTIONS

①▶ Set off along lane to L of Dog and Partridge. ②▶ At junction fork R through gate and up road to Heath Farm. At farm go straight on through gate and along cart-track. ③▶ Go through gate/stile by small buildings and forward alongside fence at edge of forest. Over stile in crossfence and walk on RH side of wall through wide gap between plantations. Cross stile onto open moor and continue up alongside wall on L. ④▶ Look for stile on L in a section of fence. At this point the right-of-way turns R and crosses the moor below the crag to gap in crosswall. Should you choose to climb to the summit, bear in mind that you're on private land. Turn R at O.S. column to walk along crest (compass bearing 60°). Through gateway in crosswall then descend steeply to rejoin right-of-way at wall corner. Turn L along old cart-track. ⑤▶ Turn R through gate by sheepfold, cross to gap in wall then down field to come alongside wall on L. Through gate and descend to farm. ⑥▶ Walk through farmyard. Just before house take gate on L then turn R to follow wall. Cross stile at wall corner and on to next farm. ⑦▶ Go through gate into farmyard and immediately turn R to pass through gap. Descend steps to cross stream by a slab bridge, then up to RH side of next farm. ⑧▶ Through gate, immediately sharp R through another gate onto access road, then turn L past end of house and forward to next house. ⑨▶ Round end of garden, through gap in wall, turn L then R along access road. Over cattle-grid and R along tarmac lane. ⑩▶ Where lane swings R go L through gate and along cart-track. Through gate into farmyard, straight on through another then bear L to fence and follow it down to gate. ⑪▶ Straight on across field to locate gate into overgrown track between fences. Cross slab bridge and forward to emerge onto farm road. Follow it down past several farms. ⑫▶ ROAD FINISH - Turn R and follow motor-road back to Tosside. For slightly longer FIELD FINISH go forward along cart-track, forking R at house. ⑬▶ Turn R in front of next house, through gate and forward with fence/hedge on R. Over stile, cross ditch and

Look for some big trout in the tiny pool under the slab bridge at Long Gill Brook.

Note the ancient milestone built into the bridge at point ⑫.

Bailey Lane can be horribly dusty in dry weather

Varied terrain, including forest roads, grassy moorland, pathless pastures and farm roads. Long, gradual and easy ascent of Whelp Stone Crag, with final steep pull of about 100' to summit (optional). No ladder-stiles, but one high and awkward wall-stile at end of walk if 'field finish' is taken. ½ mile on motor-roads if 'road finish' is used.

25

head up towards top RH corner of big field. Cross stile in wire fence to reach step-stile in wall just beyond 'Tosside' sign. Turn L along road into village.

TOSSIDE

South door, Tosside Church.

THIS REMOTE HILLSIDE VILLAGE SITS ASTRIDE THE YORKS/LANCS BORDER. THE PARISH CHURCH OF ST. BARTHOLOMEW CONTAINS SEVERAL NOTEWORTHY FEATURES. IN THE SANCTUARY ARE SOME JACOBEAN PEWS DISPLAYING THE INITIALS OF LOCAL FAMILIES. THE PULPIT IS ALSO JACOBEAN (1701). THE OCTAGONAL FONT IS INSCRIBED 'NOW THAT AL CHILDREN BAPTISED HEARE GOD GAVE THEM GOOD LIVES TO LEAD THE ETERNAL GOD TO FEARE 1619'. THE DOG AND PARTRIDGE IS A MOST EXCELLENT WATERING-HOLE.

GISBURN FOREST 🌲🌲🌲🌲🌲🌲🌲🌲🌲🌲

CONIFERS - PARTICULARLY SITKA SPRUCE - DOMINATE THESE VAST PLANTATIONS, ALTHOUGH THE FORESTRY COMMISSION IS GRADUALLY INTRODUCING MORE BROADLEAVED SPECIES. THE FOREST IS AN IDEAL HABITAT FOR SUCH INTERESTING BIRDS AS THE SPARROWHAWK, GOSHAWK, SISKIN, PIED FLYCATCHER, CROSSBILL, GOLDCREST AND ASSORTED OWLS. IT IS ALSO FREQUENTED BY THE TINY ROE DEER - REDDISH-BROWN IN SUMMER, GREY IN WINTER - WHICH LIVES HERE EITHER SINGLY OR IN SMALL GROUPS FEEDING ON LEAVES, HERBS AND BERRIES. YOU'LL BE LUCKY TO SPOT ONE, FOR IT IS AN EXTREMELY SHY, TIMID CREATURE, BUT YOU MAY WELL HEAR ITS SHORT, DEEP BARK.

WHELP STONE CRAG

This gritstone outcrop is an outstanding viewpoint, the panorama including Stocks Reservoir and the rounded fells of Bowland to the west, Pendle Hill to the south and a fine array of Dales mountains to the east beyond the A65.

Brandy, the author's Border Terrier, waits patiently whilst her master staggers up the last few feet to the summit trig. point.

O.S. MAP D

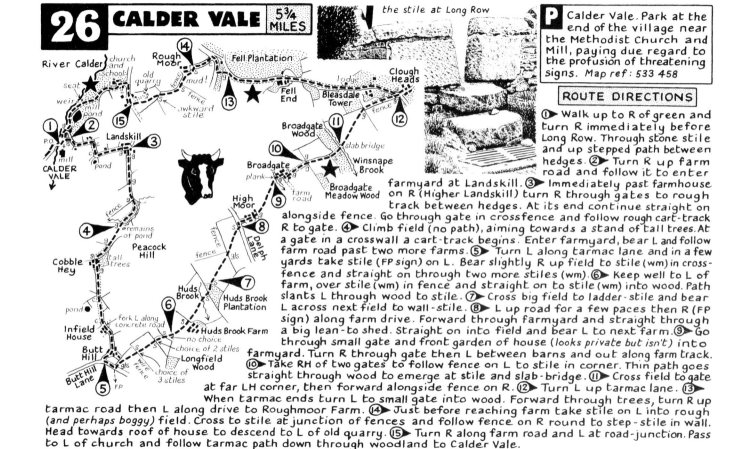

26 CALDER VALE 5¾ MILES

the stile at Long Row

ROUTE DIRECTIONS

① Walk up to R of green and turn R immediately before Long Row. Through stone stile and up stepped path between hedges. ② Turn R up farm road and follow it to enter farmyard at Landskill. ③ Immediately past farmhouse on R (Higher Landskill) turn R through gates to rough track between hedges. At its end continue straight on alongside fence. Go through gate in crossfence and follow rough cart-track R to gate. ④ Climb field (no path), aiming towards a stand of tall trees. At a gate in a crosswall a cart-track begins. Enter farmyard, bear L and follow farm road past two more farms. ⑤ Turn L along tarmac lane and in a few yards take stile (FP sign) on L. Bear slightly R up field to stile (wm) in crossfence and straight on through two more stiles (wm). ⑥ Keep well to L of farm, over stile (wm) in fence and straight on to stile (wm) into wood. Path slants L through wood to stile. ⑦ Cross big field to ladder-stile and bear L across next field to wall-stile. ⑧ L up road for a few paces then R (FP sign) along farm drive. Forward through farmyard and straight through a big lean-to shed. Straight on into field and bear L to next farm. ⑨ Go through small gate and front garden of house (*looks private but isn't*) into farmyard. Turn R through gate then L between barns and out along farm track. ⑩ Take RH of two gates to follow fence on L to stile in corner. Thin path goes straight through wood to emerge at stile and slab-bridge. ⑪ Cross field to gate at far LH corner, then forward alongside fence on R. ⑫ Turn L up tarmac lane. ⑬ When tarmac ends turn L to small gate into wood. Forward through trees, turn R up tarmac road then L along drive to Roughmoor Farm. ⑭ Just before reaching farm take stile on L into rough (*and perhaps boggy*) field. Cross to stile at junction of fences and follow fence on R round to step-stile in wall. Head towards roof of house to descend to L of old quarry. ⑮ Turn R along farm road and L at road-junction. Pass to L of church and follow tarmac path down through woodland to Calder Vale.

Very easy walking. Motor-road walking negligible. 1¼ miles on tarmac farm and estate roads, otherwise mostly pathless pastures (*which may be muddy after rain*) with small pockets of woodland. 1 ladder-stile (with adjacent gate).

THIS IS A JOURNEY WHICH GETS BETTER AND BETTER THE FURTHER YOU GO. AS FAR AS POINT ⑤ THE WALKING IS RATHER UNDISTINGUISHED. SOME ANCIENT DWELLINGS (17TH C DATESTONES) ARE PASSED, BUT THEY'RE SOMEWHAT DRAB AND UNATTRACTIVE. DURING ITS LATER STAGES, HOWEVER, THE WALK IS BLESSED WITH EXQUISITE VIEWS AND LOVELY WOODLAND.

CALDER VALE

has an air of incongruity – an industrial village in a lovely wooded setting. The cotton mill was built in 1835 by the brothers Jonathan and Richard Jackson, who were Quakers. (Another brother – John – opened a paper mill at nearby Oakenclough). The Calder Vale mill combined spinning and weaving, and was originally powered by waterwheel; the old mill pond and remains of the water-race will be passed at the end of this walk.

During the intervening years the looms have been driven in turn by turbine, beam-engine and gas-engine. The mill still flourishes, and the looms, now powered by electricity, run twenty-four hours a day seven days a week.

Calder Vale was built at the same time as the mill. Envisaged as a model village, it had a temperance hotel with a reading room, and the houses all had gardens, there being an annual competition to encourage residents to keep them in good order.

THE PARISH CHURCH OF ST. JOHN THE EVANGELIST stands in isolation high above the village. Built in 1863, it is a large, solid-looking and well cared-for building, with some particularly attractive stained-glass windows. The adjacent school was built at the same time as the church and was enlarged in 1966.

BLEASDALE TOWER

Originally a simple shooting-lodge; rebuilt and enlarged in 1847 by William James Garnett, a philanthropist and agricultural reformer. Garnett, who was MP for Lancaster 1857-64, founded the North Lancashire Reformatory School at Bleasdale in 1857, at a time when reform schools were a new concept in the handling of juvenile delinquents. Up to 125 youths were housed in the cottages at CLOUGH HEAD and were taught various skills and trades. The school closed in 1905.

THE ATTRACTIVE RIVER CALDER IS A TRIBUTARY OF THE WYRE, WHICH IT JOINS JUST SOUTH OF GARSTANG

A LAMENT...

A few waymarks would not come amiss at High Moor and Broadgate, for the route through these farmyards is by no means obvious. Sadly, this problem occurs all too frequently, yet is one which need not exist. Walkers don't like farmyards. Their general desire is to pass through as quickly and unobtrusively as possible, and so minimise the risk of being bitten by dogs, trampled by cows, gored by bulls, savaged by geese or run over by tractors. Farmers get annoyed (understandably) with walkers who stray off rights-of-way. One would therefore think that it would be in their own interest to undertake the simple task of providing a few signs. The odd arrow could save a good deal of hassle and embarrassment.

O.S.MAP E

A SOMEWHAT COMPLEX ROUTE REQUIRING CAREFUL REFERENCE TO MAP AND DIRECTIONS

P Abbeystead. At road junction on E. side of Stoops Bridge drive through the tall gateposts and park on the riverside verge.
Map ref: 563 543

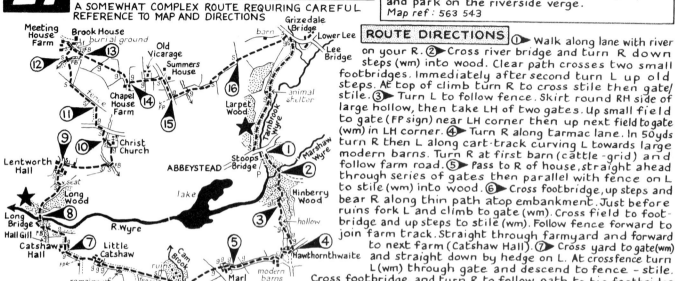

ROUTE DIRECTIONS

①▶ Walk along lane with river on your R. **②▶** Cross river bridge and turn R down steps (wm) into wood. Clear path crosses two small footbridges. Immediately after second turn L up old steps. At top of climb turn R to cross stile then gate/stile. **③▶** Turn L to follow fence. Skirt round RH side of large hollow, then take LH of two gates. Up small field to gate (FP sign) near LH corner then up next field to gate (wm) in LH corner. **④▶** Turn R along tarmac lane. In 50yds turn R then L along cart-track curving L towards large modern barns. Turn R at first barn (cattle-grid) and follow farm road. **⑤▶** Pass to R of house, straight ahead through series of gates then parallel with fence on L to stile (wm) into wood. **⑥▶** Cross footbridge, up steps and bear R along thin path atop embankment. Just before ruins fork L and climb to gate (wm). Cross field to footbridge and up steps to stile (wm). Follow fence forward to join farm track. Straight through farmyard and forward to next farm (Catshaw Hall). **⑦▶** Cross yard to gate (wm) and straight down by hedge on L. At crossfence turn L (wm) through gate and descend to fence – stile. Cross footbridge and turn R to follow path to big footbridge over Wyre. **⑧▶** Straight ahead to ladder-stile. Climb steps up wooded bank to ladder-stile, then up RH side of field and cross stile to seat. Turn L to follow fence round to farmyard. **⑨▶** At house turn R over stile (wm) and forward with wall on L. Keep straight on, aiming for distant buildings. Cross stiles and footbridge then L up to gate into churchyard. **⑩▶** Over stile in LH corner, cross slab bridge and turn R up to stile. L up road, and in 100yds take gate (FP sign) on R. Go up RH side of line of trees. **⑪▶** Follow fence to L, cross it at stile (FP sign) and head for farm. **⑫▶** Cross footbridge and wall then make for RH building to reach stile in overgrown little lane. Cross this stile to inspect buildings (see notes - Meeting House Farm) then return and follow wall to footbridge. **⑬▶** Bear L (120°) over brow of hill to locate gate (wm) in crossfence, then head for farm. **⑭▶** Don't enter farmyard. Turn L through gate (wm), cross field to small gate just below

Undulating pastures, mostly pathless but well waymarked. Easy walking through attractively wooded countryside. Road-walking negligible. Not a good walk for dogs – most of the fields have livestock and there are many stiles (including 5 ladder-stiles).

house and straight on to stile onto road. Turn R along road. ⑮▶ In 200yds take metal gate on L and follow old cart-track to gate(wm). Keep straight on to come alongside fence on L. Cross it at stile (wm) and follow it forward to ladder-stile at corner. ⑯▶ Straight on, passing well below barn, to locate marker-post and small footbridge. Descend to wall-stile onto road. Turn R through gate/ladder-stile and follow cart-track back to Stoops Bridge.

CAM BROOK AND CATSHAW

At point ⑥ we cross the mini-gorge where the lively CAM BROOK plunges down over water-worn rocks as it nears the end of its journey from the barren slopes of Hawthornthwaite Fell to the Wyre. Soon it will pass the fragmentary and overgrown ruins of CATSHAW MILL and cottages. The water-driven cotton-spinning mill was destroyed by fire in 1848. The embankment along which we approach the ruins is the remains of the mill pond. LITTLE CATSHAW (1763) and CATSHAW HALL (1678) are venerable farmsteads, the latter having once been a manor house.

Catshaw Hall

THE SHEPHERDS' CHURCH

Abbeystead's Christ Church, though rebuilt in 1733, dates back at least to the 14th C. It is known as the shepherds' church, for its stained-glass windows depict Biblical shepherd scenes and its porch has rows of hooks where visiting shepherds once hung their crooks and lanterns. Above the door is the inscription 'O ye shepherds hear the word of the Lord'. The pulpit is Jacobean (1684), and the church's most notable artefact is a copy of the 'Geneva Bible', so called because it was translated there during a period of religious persecution in 16th C. England. It is also known as the 'Breeches Bible', for in Genesis 3 v 7 the word 'aprons' is translated as 'breeches'. (In the N.E.B. the word becomes 'loincloths'.)

O.S. MAP C

MEETING HOUSE FARM

The QUAKERS, or, more correctly, the SOCIETY OF FRIENDS, had a small Meeting House here. It was behind the house on the right as you cross the stile, and is now part of it. The front part of the house was a school which was added in the late 19th C. The white house (Brook House - now greatly enlarged) was the schoolmaster's residence. From the interjacent yard a small gate gives public access to the Quaker burial ground with its simple, uniform headstones. The Society of Friends was founded by George Fox in the 17th C. Their worship stresses the freedom of all to take an active part in the service. They have no priests or ministers.

FOR NOTES ON ABBEYSTEAD AND THE RIVER WYRE SEE WALK 6

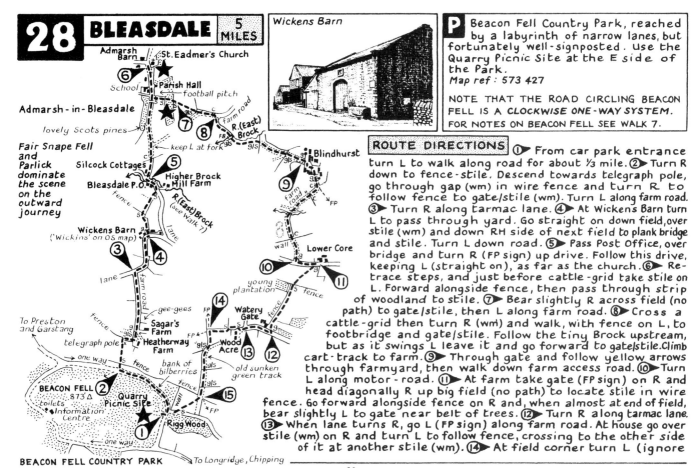

28 BLEASDALE — 5 MILES

Wickens Barn

P Beacon Fell Country Park, reached by a labyrinth of narrow lanes, but fortunately well-signposted. Use the Quarry Picnic Site at the E side of the Park.
Map ref: 573 427

NOTE THAT THE ROAD CIRCLING BEACON FELL IS A *CLOCKWISE ONE-WAY SYSTEM*.
FOR NOTES ON BEACON FELL SEE WALK 7.

ROUTE DIRECTIONS

① From car park entrance turn L to walk along road for about ⅓ mile. ② Turn R down to fence-stile. Descend towards telegraph pole, go through gap (wm) in wire fence and turn R to follow fence to gate/stile (wm). Turn L along farm road. ③ Turn R along tarmac lane. ④ At Wickens Barn turn L to pass through yard. Go straight on down field, over stile (wm) and down RH side of next field to plank bridge and stile. Turn L down road. ⑤ Pass Post Office, over bridge and turn R (FP sign) up drive. Follow this drive, keeping L (straight on), as far as the church. ⑥ Retrace steps, and just before cattle-grid take stile on L. Forward alongside fence, then pass through strip of woodland to stile. ⑦ Bear slightly R across field (no path) to gate/stile, then L along farm road. ⑧ Cross a cattle-grid then turn R (wm) and walk, with fence on L, to footbridge and gate/stile. Follow the tiny Brock upstream, but as it swings L leave it and go forward to gate/stile. Climb cart-track to farm. ⑨ Through gate and follow yellow arrows through farmyard, then walk down farm access road. ⑩ Turn L along motor-road. ⑪ At farm take gate (FP sign) on R and head diagonally R up big field (no path) to locate stile in wire fence. Go forward alongside fence on R and, when almost at end of field, bear slightly L to gate near belt of trees. ⑫ Turn R along tarmac lane. ⑬ When lane turns R, go L (FP sign) along farm road. At house go over stile (wm) on R and turn L to follow fence, crossing to the other side of it at another stile (wm). ⑭ At field corner turn L (ignore

Easy walking on lanes, farm roads and pathless pastures. One mile on very quiet motor-roads. No ladder-stiles. Best done in dry weather; after rain you will encounter muddy sections - particularly on the return route.

28

stiles) and climb to gate/stile at top of field. Turn R up an old, sunken cart-track. ⑮▶ When fence on R ends, turn ½ R to go diagonally up field to stile at LH end of wall. Turn R up lane.

BLEASDALE

Bleasdale School

is a green and pleasant valley sheltered to the north by a mass of high fells. Its rural community, though widely scattered, manages nevertheless to sustain a Church, Parish Hall, School and, at HIGHER BROCK MILL (now converted into attractive properties), a Post Office-cum-café✽ occupying premises which were once a blacksmith's forge. By the Parish Hall stands an information plaque giving details of BLEASDALE CIRCLE, the site of an early-Bronze Age village dating from around 1850 BC. A visit will entail a short extension to the walk, and permission must be obtained (see details on plaque).

✽ *the Post Office is in the adjoining parish of Goosnargh*

BLINDHURST

is a striking and most beautifully maintained black and white farm-house. It has a 1731 datestone and an unusual pillared Georgian doorway. The name 'Blindhurst' means 'a dark or obscure wood'.

Look out for hares in the fields around Blindhurst.

ST. EADMER'S CHURCH

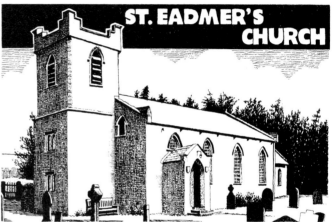

THIS REMOTE LITTLE CHURCH AT ADMARSH-IN-BLEASDALE IS THOUGHT TO BE THE ONLY ONE IN CHRISTENDOM DEDICATED TO ST. EADMER, WHICH IS SCARCELY SURPRISING, FOR EADMER WAS SUCH AN OBSCURE SAINT THAT NO-ONE SEEMS TO BE QUITE SURE WHO HE ACTUALLY WAS! A CHAPEL IS KNOWN TO HAVE EXISTED IN BLEASDALE SINCE THE REIGN OF ELIZABETH I, AND THE PRESENT CHURCH (BUILT 1835) MAY OCCUPY THE SITE OF THE OLDER ONE, THOUGH SOME SUGGEST THAT THE NEARBY ADMARSH BARN WAS EITHER THE ORIGINAL CHURCH OR ON THE SITE OF IT. TWO WINDOWS FROM THE OLD CHAPEL ARE BUILT INTO THE TOWER.

O.S. MAP E

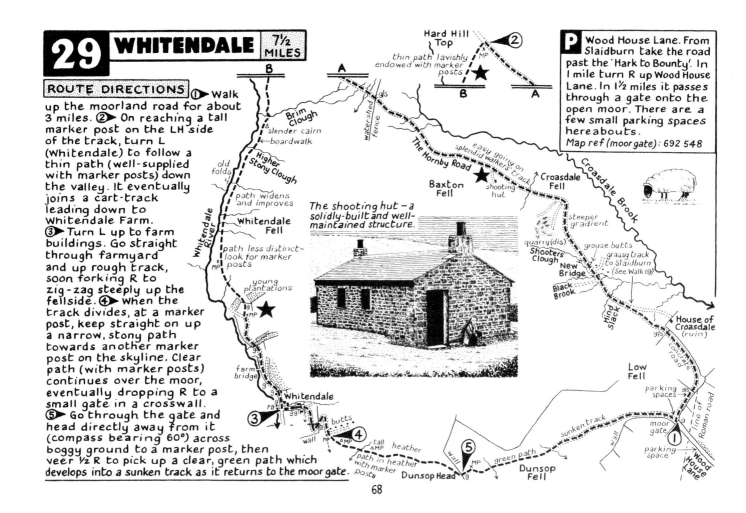

29 WHITENDALE 7½ MILES

ROUTE DIRECTIONS

① Walk up the moorland road for about 3 miles. ② On reaching a tall marker post on the LH side of the track, turn L (Whitendale) to follow a thin path (well-supplied with marker posts) down the valley. It eventually joins a cart-track leading down to Whitendale Farm. ③ Turn L up to farm buildings. Go straight through farmyard and up rough track, soon forking R to zig-zag steeply up the fellside. ④ When the track divides, at a marker post, keep straight on up a narrow, stony path towards another marker post on the skyline. Clear path (with marker posts) continues over the moor, eventually dropping R to a small gate in a crosswall. ⑤ Go through the gate and head directly away from it (compass bearing 60°) across boggy ground to a marker post, then veer ½ R to pick up a clear, green path which develops into a sunken track as it returns to the moor gate.

P Wood House Lane. From Slaidburn take the road past the 'Hark to Bounty'. In 1 mile turn R up Wood House Lane. In 1½ miles it passes through a gate onto the open moor. There are a few small parking spaces hereabouts.
Map ref (moor gate): 692 548

Hard Hill Top

thin path lavishly endowed with marker posts

Brim Clough

slender cairn
boardwalk

Higher Stony Clough

old folds

watershed fence

The Hornby Road

easy going on splendid walkers' track

Baxton Fell

shooting hut

Croasdale Fell

Croasdale Brook

steeper gradient

quarry (dis)

grouse butts

Shooters Clough

New Bridge

grassy track to Slaidburn (see Walk 19)

Black Brook

Whitendale River

path widens and improves

Whitendale Fell

path less distinct — look for marker posts

young plantations

The shooting hut – a solidly-built and well-maintained structure.

farm bridge

Whitendale

FB

butts

wall

tall heather

path in heather with marker posts

Dunsop Head

Dunsop Fell

green path

Low Fell

parking spaces

House of Croasdale (ruin)

Hind Slack

sunken track

parking space

moor gate

Wood House Lane

line of Roman road

68

Exposed moorland walking on good tracks and waymarked paths. 1190' of ascent, mostly on gentle gradients but with one steep climb of some 430' from Whitendale Farm. Some wet ground in upper Whitendale and around Dunsop Head. No motor-roads. 1 ladder-stile (with adjacent gate).

29

WHITENDALE

Whitendale — farmhouse and Keepers Cottage

THE LIVELY WHITENDALE RIVER FLOWS THROUGH A DEEP VALLEY BEFORE JOINING FORCES WITH THE BRENNAND RIVER TO FORM THE RIVER DUNSOP (*See Walk 8*). UPPER WHITENDALE IS BLEAK INDEED, BUT THE TINY HAMLET OF WHITENDALE NESTLES IN AN ARBOREAL SETTING OF SUPREME BEAUTY, AND THE FARM, DESPITE ITS REMOTENESS, LOOKS WELL-TENDED AND PROSPEROUS. THE MAIN FARMHOUSE WAS BUILT BY THE UBIQUITOUS TOWNELEYS IN 1854. THE PICTURESQUE KEEPERS COTTAGE STILL RETAINS A MULLION SILL AND TOPSTONE.

THE HORNBY ROAD

Overlaying a Roman road in places, and alternatively known as 'The Salter's Way', this is one of the country's finest moorland tracks. A packhorse route of great antiquity, it was used for the transport of salt from Morecambe Bay to the farms of Bowland and the Ribble Valley.

BIRDS OF THE MOOR

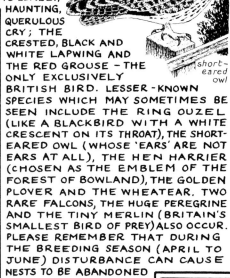

short-eared owl

THESE WILD UPLANDS MAKE AN IDEAL HABITAT FOR MANY SPECIES OF BIRD, PROVIDING THEM WITH NESTING-SITES, COVER AND FOOD SUPPLIES. FAMILIAR TO ALL WALKERS WILL BE THE LONG-BILLED CURLEW, WITH ITS LONELY, HAUNTING, QUERULOUS CRY; THE CRESTED, BLACK AND WHITE LAPWING AND THE RED GROUSE — THE ONLY EXCLUSIVELY BRITISH BIRD. LESSER-KNOWN SPECIES WHICH MAY SOMETIMES BE SEEN INCLUDE THE RING OUZEL (LIKE A BLACKBIRD WITH A WHITE CRESCENT ON ITS THROAT), THE SHORT-EARED OWL (WHOSE 'EARS' ARE NOT EARS AT ALL), THE HEN HARRIER (CHOSEN AS THE EMBLEM OF THE FOREST OF BOWLAND), THE GOLDEN PLOVER AND THE WHEATEAR. TWO RARE FALCONS, THE HUGE PEREGRINE AND THE TINY MERLIN (BRITAIN'S SMALLEST BIRD OF PREY) ALSO OCCUR. PLEASE REMEMBER THAT DURING THE BREEDING SEASON (APRIL TO JUNE) DISTURBANCE CAN CAUSE NESTS TO BE ABANDONED AND CHICKS TO DIE.

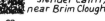

'slender cairn', near Brim Clough

O.S. MAP D

30 LUNESIDE PATHS — 7¼ MILES

ROUTE DIRECTIONS

P Crook o' Lune Picnic Site, signposted from the A683 just W of Caton. Map ref: 521 648

① Go down path from front corner of car park (FP to Picnic Site). Take 3rd path on L (down steps – SP Lune Valley Ramble). Keep R at fork to gate and riverside path. Just beyond a weir the path crosses a stile into woodland. ② On leaving wood bear slightly L across field to footbridge, then pass waterworks bridge to stile into woodland. ③ Leave wood at a stile and turn R to follow river bank around a huge bend. ④ Turn L (wm) to pass to R of barn and on to gate/stile. Bear R, skirting edge of depression, then head towards roof of distant barn to eventually re-join river bank. ⑤ At a gate/stile (wm) join a cart-track. After passing buildings it becomes a steeply rising tarmac lane. Straight on at village crossroads. ⑥ Turn L over iron ladder-stile (FP sign) and pass RH end of hedge to gate/stile (wm). Climb to iron ladder-stile (80 yds to R of wood) then on to iron ladder-stile to L of farm. Follow fence/hedge on R to next farm. ⑦ Middle Highfield is a complicated hotch-potch, and finding your way through it is no mean feat. Enter the yard, pass in front of the house and go through the gate adjoining its corner. Go forward to a stone stile to pass immediately to the R of the second house. Climb another stone stile, then turn L to pass around the LH end of the buildings. Turn R down to a gate set at right-angles to a high wall. ⑧ Follow wall forward, over ladder-stile (wm), through gate (wm) in hedge and down field to gate (wm) at its bottom LH corner. ⑨ Descend to farmyard, turn L (wm) down to gate (wm), then on through gateway to swing-gate (wm) into wood. Follow clear path through wood to swing-gate (wm). ⑩ Go to hedge-corner (wm) and follow hedge forward. ⑪ At stone stile (wm) go through hedge and turn L down to stile at RH end of building. Turn R

The Lune is known as the 'Queen of Lancashire rivers,' and the walk from Crook o' Lune to Aughton takes us along one of its loveliest stretches. From February to October you are likely to see anglers, often waist-deep in water, casting with fly, worm or spinner for the salmon for which the Lune is famous.

Ox-eye daisy flowers in the riverside meadows June to August

Map labels:
High Barn (posh residence)
Far Highfield 1687
Aughton
seat (phew!)
Burton House
Middle Highfield
hedge
redundant ladder-stile
fence
steep pull
high wall
gatepost with benchmark
barn
Lower Highfield
cart-track
Burton Wood (Nature Reserve)
Lawson's Wood
Halton Park Farm
aqueduct
Over Lune Barn
mound
mound
ruined wall
copse
Artle Beck
R. Lune
Park Lane
weir
car park, toilets
Caton Low Mill
Crook o' Lune
to Caton
to Lancaster
A683
no path

Steepish tarmac lane up to Aughton, otherwise very easy walking. The riverside woodland paths tend to be slippery after rain. Most of the return route via the Highfields is pathless, but there are plenty of waymarks except at the one place where they are most needed – Middle Highfield. The comments made in Walk 26 (A Lament) apply here also. 4 ladder-stiles (3 of which are low, iron ones). 1 mile on very quiet motor-roads.

down farm road. ⑫▶ Turn L along tarmac lane. ⑬▶ Turn L along road, and after about 200yds forsake the narrow pavement in favour of a grass path running behind the wall all the way back to the car park.

CROOK o' LUNE

Crook o' Lune has long been a popular beauty-spot. The scenery moved the poet Thomas Gray (1716-71) to write, 'Every feature which constitutes a perfect landscape of the extensive sort, is here not only boldly – marked, but also in its best position'. The famous landscape painter J.M.W. Turner (1775-1851) also found inspiration here, and in 1818 produced a watercolour which now hangs in the Courtauld Institute of Art in London. The iron bridges across the neck of the great bend in the Lune were constructed to carry the Lancaster to Wennington railway, which opened in 1849. The line was notoriously inefficient and badly-organised, but managed to operate until 1966, when the dreaded Dr. Beeching wielded his mighty axe.

CATON LOW MILL WAS A WATER-POWERED COTTON MILL BUILT IN 1783. IN THOSE DAYS PROBABLY ABOUT ⅔ OF THE WORKFORCE WOULD BE CHILDREN, AND THE REST MOSTLY WOMEN. THE MILL OPERATED UNTIL THE 1970s.

Approaching the gate at point ⑩. If you've done all these walks in numerical sequence, without ever getting lost, you have now covered 189¾ miles and have 1½ miles to go.

O.S. MAP A

TWO STYLES OF STILE

This iron ladder-stile is one of a series between Aughton and Middle Highfield. The removal of field boundaries has rendered some of them obsolete.

A more conventional stone gap-stile at point ⑪ – waymarked and daubed with white paint.

● THE AQUEDUCT was built in 1906 and carries a pipeline which brings water the 95 miles from Thirlmere, in the Lake District, to Manchester.
● The ancient BURTON WOOD once provided charcoal for iron-smelting. It is now a nature reserve managed by the Lancashire Wildlife Trust.
● The river here is rich in BIRDLIFE. Look out for dipper, kingfisher, oystercatcher, various wagtails, heron and shelduck. The latter is a large, goose-like duck; mainly white with a dark-green head, some black markings and a rust-coloured breastband. It often nests in old rabbit-burrows, sometimes a considerable distance from water.

shelduck

SYMBOLS USED ON THE MAPS

The maps are based on the O.S. Pathfinder Series (1 : 25 000)

■ church with tower
● church with spire
+ church or chapel without either

 buildings
 crags
 woods, forests
 lakes, reservoirs

Route (not necessarily a visible path)

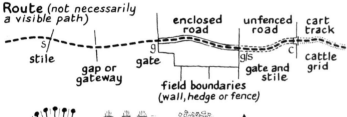

enclosed road

unfenced road

cart track

S stile

gap or gateway

g gate

field boundaries (wall, hedge or fence)

g/s gate and stile

c cattle grid

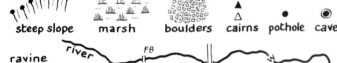

steep slope   marsh   boulders   cairns   pothole   cave

ravine   river   stream   FB footbridge   bridge   waterfall   direction of flow

BS boundary stone   MS milestone
GP guidepost   MP marker post   PO Post Office

★ the best places on the walk (in the author's opinion)

ABBREVIATIONS USED IN THE TEXT

R right   L left   RH right-hand   LH left-hand   FP footpath
BW bridleway   SP signpost   wm waymarked

PLEASE OBSERVE THE **COUNTRY CODE**

- Enjoy the countryside and respect its life and work
- Use gates and stiles to cross walls and fences
- Keep your dog under close control
- Protect wildlife, plants and trees
- Help to keep all water clean
- Make no unnecessary noise
- Fasten all gates
- Leave livestock, crops and machinery alone
- Keep to public paths across farmland
- Take special care on country roads
- Guard against all risk of fire
- Leave no litter